Life
in the
Blue
ZONE

God, I Didn't
See This Coming

Why should a Christ follower be scared of heaven?

JIM BURTON

Life in the Blue Zone: God I didn't see this coming
© Copyright 2014 Jim Burton

First Print Edition 2014

Cover Design by Jeff Hatcher

Published in the United States of America

Contents

Foreword

IN 2002 WHEN OUR FAMILY faced one of the most feared and difficult challenges in life—cancer—the range of emotions stretched from sublime to absolute dread. Cancer evoked many of our greatest fears, never realizing that it would also test the depth of our character and convictions.

Our family survived cancer and enjoyed more than a decade without a major health challenge. Then in 2013, amyotrophic lateral sclerosis (ALS), or Lou Gehrig's disease, became a new reality for us.

Life in the Blue Zone: God, I Didn't See This Coming is for those who receive a challenging—perhaps life threatening—health diagnosis. This book is also for their family and friends as many questions emerge. Beyond the barrage of med talk and options that suddenly seem to become the center of a patient's life, there will be lingering spiritual questions including "why me?"

Each year in the United States, about 1.3 million people receive a cancer diagnosis. Nearly 600,000 Americans die from cancer each year. Cancer is the cause of one out of every four deaths in the United States. As startling as those statistics might be, there's hope as America has nearly nine million cancer survivors alive today.

ALS is rare. An estimated 5,600 people learn each year that they have ALS, according to the ALS Association. Unlike cancer, which claims fewer lives today than previously, ALS is terminal. The standard prognosis is that the patient will live three to five years following onset of the disease.

You're much more than a statistic. To your family and friends, you're an important part of their life. They want to be supportive, and you'll need their support.

At some point in a difficult health journey, you'll probably talk to God. That prayer might happen in anger or disgust, particularly at first. A major illness forces deep spiritual questions that flow much more quickly than do the answers. Eventually, you'll likely desire God's blessing as you ask for understanding and healing.

In some ways, *Life in the Blue Zone* is three books. First, it is the testimony of one family that faced two major illnesses. Every family will have a different story, and our experience may not be the best model of response. We simply share what happened to us and with us. Second, the book is a theological example of God's sovereignty with life principles that teach us about faith, healing, and holiness. Third, it's a prayer plan to help people pray for friends and loved ones facing tough health issues. The sequence follows my family's experience as we faced the shock of cancer and later an ALS diagnosis and all the inherent fears that accompany both, the spiritual journey that took place in the midst of the battles, and the results of the experiences.

The heart of *Life in the Blue Zone* is the seven-point prayer plan to direct your prayers for healing. I encourage you to use the prayer plan daily as you face cancer, ALS, strokes, paralysis, or any disease and its consequences.

Why would you need a prayer plan? A prayer plan is simply an outline for directed prayer to address a particular concern. Scripture is the foundation for this prayer plan as it focuses on passages about healing. Besides the seven passages in this prayer plan, an Appendix lists many other passages that you can use to direct your prayer for healing.

Perhaps the most important prayers for healing offered on your behalf will be yours. That's why it's so important that you make a commitment to pray regularly. Effective prayer requires regimen and discipline. Don't hesitate to ask others to pray for you, but be willing to do the same for yourself.

Patients need the support of others, particularly those who will pray. This prayer plan is also for those whom you would invite to pray for you. Your friends and family can use this outline to pray specifically for you.

One of the first things to learn with a critical illness is that it becomes what you make it. For instance, a major health issue has the power to clobber you with depression or become an instrument in God's hand to bring a fresh perspective to life, making life more precious and useable for God's glory. By committing to a prayer plan for healing, you can take the first step toward making the illness your ally and not your enemy.

This book won't serve as a simple formula with a quick-fix guarantee. Nor am I naïve to the reality of terminal diagnoses that many patients face and all the heartache that entails. However, even when facing a terminal diagnosis, *Life in the Blue Zone* may be a tool that helps you understand the spiritual dimensions of your life, your illness, and eternity. God is always at work in your life, both when you're sick and well. No diagnosis is too big for God.

Why is the focus primarily on cancer and ALS when so many chronic diseases and other tragedies exist today? While the principles in *Life in the Blue Zone* would apply to any health challenge, I can speak best to the issue of healing from our family's experiences.

No one wants to park in the blue zone as no one wants to be sick or disabled. However, my prayer is that our family's experience with cancer and ALS will encourage you and others when faced with a dreaded diagnosis. In the end, we pray that you, too, will discover God's blessing in the blue zone.

Jim Burton

PART ONE

Chapter One

How will this change you?

"SIT DOWN."

It took about one nanosecond for those words to get my attention. In the nearly thirty years of our dating and marriage, my bride had given me very few imperatives. This was bigger than "take out the trash," or "pick up the kids." Though she has a flare for the dramatic and is one of the most entertaining and hilarious people I've ever known, this was absolutely serious. The tone of her voice communicated one-hundred times more than her choice of words. In the midst of yet another chaotic night in the suburban life of an American family with two teenagers, my wife had something to say. She wasn't interested in my tendency to take charge and fix our hectic agendas. The podium of our life was now hers.

Our oldest son's high school soccer team had just lost 5-4 in a regular-season game to the number one team in the state. He plays goalkeeper. Few parents should ever experience that torture. Emotions had run high all night. Our son blamed himself entirely for the loss. His pain, as you might guess, was especially his mother's pain. This was a tough night at the Burton home when a familiar, calm, and firm voice began to put everything in perspective.

I had absolutely no idea what was coming, but I knew it was big. It's amazing what your mind can process in such a short moment. Divorce? No. We're both first-born children, and we often kidded that we were each too stubborn to give the other one any relief. Parents? Our parents were in their seventies. My mother was already suffering from advanced Alzheimer's disease. Maybe someone else was sick. Siblings? Kim and I have five siblings between us. We dearly love each one and the spouses of those whom they married. Maybe something had happened to one of them. Neighbors? Church? What?

Earlier that day, Kim had gone for a follow-up mammogram. What had appeared as a small "something" in November that wasn't anything to worry about was two tumors in March, one at least an inch long. The radiologist's words to her had been, "It looks bad."

My wife had my attention. It was perhaps as undivided and focused as any other time in our relationship. Suddenly, soccer games, schedules, and business travel weren't nearly as important as they'd been moments earlier. Up until that moment, I would've sworn to you that Kim was the most important person in my life, and that I loved her more than any other person on the face of this earth did. I would also honestly have had to admit that my actions and decisions probably rarely reflected that. As a workaholic who felt the pressure of provision for my family, too many things had been getting in the way of what could easily have been a more dynamic relationship. On that night, what I felt for my wife was a depth of emotion that she had deserved to feel everyday of our marriage. Beyond a doubt, she was now number one—not the boys or me. The spotlight had to shift to her. I was ready to do whatever it took to protect her and save her from the potential time bomb in her body.

Kim would later record in her journal that I had "pain and fear on my face" that night. So much for being steady, strong, and collected. Her news scared me. The anxiety of incomplete information can be worse than the truth. Too many possibilities and questions start racing through your head, bouncing around like pin balls with no apparent direction or entirely predictable course. Lights and whistles were going off in a sudden rush of private emotional chaos.

We had few answers that night. Two days later, we were in the office of a general surgeon. Kim had worked eighteen years in surgery as a certified surgical technologist so she knew the language, procedures, and options. As Kim and the doctor jumped into their med talk, I sat in the corner and watched them volley back and forth like a tennis match wondering what in the world they were saying. Lumpectomies, mastectomies, implants, tram flaps, chemotherapy, radiation—these represented possibilities. Until we had a lab report, these were merely possible choices on a road we'd just as soon not travel. So I raised my hand. "Excuse me, but everything I know about breast cancer I learned last night on the Internet. And the Internet says that when there is more than one lump, lumpectomies are rarely an option. Whether this is cancer or not, aren't we looking at a big surgery? Don't we want these masses out of her body?"

The answers were yes. No matter what we would later learn from lab reports, Kim was going to have surgery.

Two days later on our oldest son's seventeenth birthday, Kim had a needle core biopsy with ultrasound. In that procedure, doctors said they found another tumor. Now there were supposedly three.

We had an anxious weekend awaiting the test results on Monday. The boys were attending a church youth retreat, so we had time alone together. That helped some. Still, we were anxious.

Then Kim took the call late Monday afternoon, and we could no longer deny our greatest fear. The doctor confirmed that Kim had cancer.

The impossible possibility had landed in our family much sooner than we would have ever expected. Kim was in her mid forties. These were good years. She looked and felt fine. Isn't this supposed to happen a little later in life?

By that time, I had learned a few more things about breast cancer. An estimated 239,000 women get this news each year. More than 120 die each day in the United States from breast cancer. Breast cancer is no respecter of age. It can strike either gender at any time, though risks do increase with age, particularly among women after the age of 35.

A husband never realizes how inadequate he is until a time like this. As a protector and provider, I desperately wanted to fix this now, but there wasn't a tool in our garage that would help Kim with cancer. Many realities quickly sink in with a cancer diagnosis, and one clear reality is that there wasn't enough time for me to run to medical school and learn surgery and oncology. She was facing the biggest questions of her life, and the medical answers weren't going to come from me. The feelings of insufficiency were at times as daunting as the diagnosis. That reality is tough for a male who thrives on being competent. The Goliath in me took a big fall. There didn't seem to be a shield big enough that I could hold in front of my bride.

Fortunately, besides the seemingly unconquerable Goliath that each man thinks he is, there is also a David in each of us. Small, inexperienced, and seemingly inadequate, facing an invisible Philistine army, the David in me took the only possible tools left and put them to use. The smooth stones in my sling were hugs and prayers. The prayers were simple as I found myself pleading with God on Kim's behalf. Even as Moses cried out to God on behalf of Miriam, his sister, who was suddenly stricken with leprosy in Numbers 12:13, my prayers were simple, "Please heal her." The pleading flowed naturally out of shock, fear, and uncertainty.

Emotionally, Kim did well, breaking down the most when she called to tell her mother. She even told her mother, "I'm sorry."

Sorry! Why would you apologize for being a victim? She didn't drink herself into this condition. There is no reasonable conclusion about any behavior a woman might engage in that would cause breast cancer. Breast cancer is practically a no-fault affliction.

But that's Kim. She never wants to be a bother. She didn't want to make her mother cry that day. She didn't want to be the center of other people's attention. Kim is the one who serves others, writes cards, cooks meals, and encourages. Servers are the hardest people in the world to serve, and she was sorry to be causing anyone else concern.

I did most of my crying on Windward. In the mornings as I drove alone to work, it would hit me somewhere along Windward Parkway, a major thoroughfare in our area. The Christian radio music I normally listened to had deeper meaning in those days. In the solitude of the commute as I listened to the music and inevitably asked the why and what-if questions, emotion would hit me. Though doctors had told us that the next two years would be difficult, and that this was probably not life threatening, I feared losing her. Through the years, I had heard so many stories of surprise with cancer. "The surgeon opened up the patient and just closed 'em back up. The cancer was spread too far." Would there be a surprise here? How would I raise my boys alone? Kim and I started dating when we were fifteen and seventeen. I couldn't imagine life without her. Then out of nowhere, tears would fill my eyes as my jaw tightened, and my breathing seemed to stagger. This was scary stuff, and it was way out of my hands.

For the next few days, I became numb. My staff at work knew something was up, but gave me the space I needed. Frankly, I wasn't very productive. I worked in a mission ministry, which was both important and very satisfying. As a worker, I loved my vocation. I had poured the last sixteen years of my life into this ministry. In my heart, I knew that life couldn't stop. This ministry was too important to suffer disruption due to my family. But my role was about to change, as were my priorities.

Family talk

The time came to tell our teen-aged boys. The night we got the lab results, there was another out-of-town soccer game. Kim stayed home with our youngest son, Jacob, and I attended the game. Our oldest son, Jim, got to the house late. I had told him after the game to hurry home; we were going to have a family meeting. "About what?" he asked in the midst of teammates walking off the field. "Life," I said.

Our family tried to pray together regularly at night. That discipline was a hard commitment to keep with my travel and the boy's schedules. So when we sat them down, they probably thought it was just another family prayer time.

As Kim began to explain, I noticed she was having trouble saying cancer. She wasn't in denial, but her nature is not to alarm or hurt other people. Our oldest, who is very straight up with his prophetic, black-and-white outlook on life finally asked her, "Is it cancer?"

Kim hesitated as she tried to prepare for a soft landing. The words weren't coming to her, so I answered the question: "Yes, your mother has cancer."

"Are you going to die?" Jacob asked.

No, there was no immediate indication that this was life threatening, just life altering.

There were a few more questions. Then Jacob, our youngest, asked the hardest question of all. "How will this change you?"

The question about knocked me out of my seat. Not even at age thirteen could he understand the depths of that probe. Though he was inquiring about the physical aspects of what lay ahead, our intuitive child with the gift of mercy was confronting us with reality. Life as we knew it was about to change for everyone, but especially for Kim. Physically and emotionally, everything was on the table.

That question became the theme of our journey. How would

this change us? The appropriate follow-up question is, "Would we let this change us—preferably for the better?"

The change had already begun. Communication between Kim and me had improved 1,000 percent, primarily because I was listening better. Suddenly, everything on my calendar wasn't nearly as important as it had been. I cancelled my plans to attend an annual meeting my team sponsored with more than 200 constituents, one I'd never missed, and one of the most important of the year. I cancelled two West Coast trips and attending an annual convention that I routinely worked. The summer was the busiest time for my ministry. The previous summer I visited more than nine cities in eight weeks. That wouldn't be happening this next summer. By June 1, we anticipated that Kim could begin chemotherapy following her healing from surgery. This journey wasn't a short trip. It would be a trek.

Within a week, we were meeting with a plastic surgeon and settling on the plan of action that Kim wanted. We were ready to attack this problem that day. However, scheduling didn't permit the surgery for another nineteen days. That curve ball broke harder than the cancer diagnosis. We anticipated the diagnosis, but we didn't anticipate having to wait. Receiving that news was like being all dressed up with nowhere to go. Now, we had to settle back into normal routines for more than two weeks. That's not easy for baby boomers. We want our hamburgers, and we want them fast. We want our printed photographs in an hour, not three days. And we want our health now, not later.

The classroom of life had just gotten bigger. There were some new lessons to learn, and some old ones to recall. One of the hardest is waiting, particularly on God. What's going on here, God? What's the point? What are you trying to teach us?

Heart issue first

I don't just love my wife. I'm proud of her. Never had I been prouder than in the early days of this challenge. She knew from the earliest moments that the biggest issue was faithfulness to God. This challenge was a *heart* issue first and a *health* issue second. Admittedly, her heart was troubled but calm as she kept the doubts and questions in check. Her relationship with God had depth before this crisis. Fortunately, her wells of faith are deep, and they're rich with fresh, cool spring water.

We both did what comes very natural at a time like this. We each turned to Scripture. Kim was looking for comfort, and I was looking for answers. When measuring strengths, I am first a learner. When measuring spiritual gifts, my primary gift is teaching. So when I want to know what's up with that, I hit the books. This challenge was going to take us to new depths of prayer, faith, and healing. We believed in the power of intercessory prayer. We believed also that prayer must be informed, intentional, and grounded in Scripture. I had developed prayer plans before related to my vocational ministry, and God clearly laid it on my heart to do that again. This prayer plan was for Kim's healing, a plan that hopefully could be shared with others who face cancer.

There was a more practical reason why I needed a prayer plan. The discipline of prayer has always been hard for me. By no means am I a "prayer warrior." Yet the challenge in our family meant that I had to step up to the plate. The responsibility to pray for Kim belonged first with me. Why should I ask others to do something for my wife that I wasn't doing or willing to do? Still, I was feeling very inadequate on the doorstep of this journey. So for me, the answer was to find Scripture about healing and to let that be my guide.

Healing is a confusing subject. In some circles, healing looks like a made-for-television circus event. In others, it's much more quiet and calm. What does Scripture teach about healing? Do New Testament-type miracles still happen? If they do, when do they happen? Why doesn't every petition for divine intervention lead to miraculous results?

Closer to home, the question was what will happen to Kim? Why was this happening to Kim? What's the purpose of this challenge for Kim's life and our family.

Chapter Two

This Is War

SHORTLY AFTER RECEIVING all of the pathology reports, we understood that Kim's cancer was life altering, not life threatening. Early detection, coupled with quick action, could stop the cancer. What we didn't know then was that weapons of the cancer battle could kill her.

When we received the pathology reports that said Kim had a speck of cancer in one lymph node, that opened up a completely new playbook. As one physician said to me, "Contrary to what most men think, a woman's breast is not a vital organ." The challenge for oncologists is that breast cancer tends to transmit cancer cells throughout the body. Where those cells park can become a haven of havoc. Early detection through self-exam, mammograms, blood work, or other means shouldn't be an option for any woman.

Kim had the advantage of early detection and an amazing medical team. However, that speck of cancer meant she would need to face the rigors of chemotherapy. Compared to her chemo journey, the modified radical mastectomy with immediate reconstruction followed by multiple other smaller procedures was a cakewalk.

The term modern medicine doesn't mean that medicine is

complete or all knowing. Modern medicine simply means that the medical profession is offering you the best knowledge they have at the time. Doctors aren't God. They have limited knowledge. However, we found them genuinely interested in Kim's health, healing, and recovery.

Curing cancer is much like solving a complicated riddle. You have all sorts of ideas about what the answer might be, but landing on the right answer is often elusive. Meanwhile, cancer is changing. The cells mutate and create new challenges for science. You might conquer the enemy in front of you, only to learn that you have more enemies on your sides and behind you. The journey is a war that one must fight on all fronts.

As much as any physician, oncologists play the odds. They know their drugs and survival rates. If you go this route, they will tell you that the chances of reoccurrence are only 5 percent. If you choose this treatment plan, your chances of reoccurrence are 10 percent. In short, most cancer patients have options, and they must learn about those options to make an informed choice with their physician.

At the time of Kim's cancer, there was an experimental treatment called Herceptin. That drug promised lesser side effects, but it required weekly chemo treatments for about a year. Kim's chemo treatment would be starting the summer before our oldest son's senior year in high school. As usual, Kim was more concerned about others than herself. She based her decision about a chemo regimen on how it would affect others, particularly our oldest son. Instead of fifty-two treatments, she chose what was the current standard, four treatments of Adriamycin-Cytoxan, followed by four with Taxotere. Administered intravenously through a huge syringe filled with red-colored chemo drugs, doctors and nurses commonly and appropriately call Adriamycin "the red devil." The drug is harsh and generates the common side effects one associates with chemo, including nausea and hair loss.

The red devil unleashed its fury on Kim. She entered the chemo phase with the best attitude possible. If attitude alone could cure cancer, Kim would've never gotten sick. But chemotherapy introduces harsh chemicals into your body. The medicine kills good and bad cells, and it can create all sorts of complications.

Our next-door neighbor had a child who expressed confusion about Kim's troubles with chemotherapy. "I never heard of a medicine that makes you sick," he said. Unfortunately, chemotherapy can cause sickness.

The chemotherapy phase of cancer is a series of actions and reactions. A patient takes chemo drugs to get well, but gets sick. Then the patient takes more drugs to respond to the sickness. That response can initiate even more reaction. The oncologists have a huge arsenal of drugs, and finding the right one is much like finding a needle in a haystack.

Kim's response to the red devil was so severe that she became dehydrated and disoriented. During an unscheduled visit to take intravenous fluids, the medical staff drew blood and ran lab reports. One of her body's chemicals was way out of kilter, which explained her lethargy and other behaviors. A nurse practitioner told me, "If we can't get this straightened out, she could die."

Die! We've gone from life-altering cancer to life-threatening chemotherapy. Nothing was making sense.

"Lord, I could use a little help here."

Clearly, stabilizing Kim's health became the objective. We made multiple visits—including weekends—to an infusion center so that she could receive more intravenous fluids and meds. We even spent our anniversary there. If that sounds like a bummer, please know that it wasn't. Kim was getting better. Nothing else mattered.

No more red devil

After three rounds of the red devil, Kim decided she wasn't going to wrestle that demon any more. I certainly agreed. We met with her lead oncologist, who had drawn the same conclusion. The oncologist wanted to stop all chemotherapy based upon the trouble Kim was having with the treatment. We said no. Our objective was to give Kim the best chance possible to beat cancer. She was willing to start the Taxotere treatment after some rest.

That respite gave us much hope. Kim became herself again. Some degree of normalcy returned to our home. We got a glimpse of life after chemo.

The remaining four treatments were mild compared to the red devil. Nausea was not an issue, but the Taxotere did cause much pain. Her bones would hurt. One day she said that even her teeth hurt. But anything was better than the nausea and disorientation that occurred with the first round.

Within two weeks of Kim's first chemotherapy treatment, her hair had started to fall out in clumps. When we met as teenagers, she had long, blond hair flowing down her back. Through the years, she had a variety of shorter hairstyles. Though difficult to face, she quickly made the decision that it was time to have her head shaved.

Nothing is easy about the cancer journey. This is war, and war is emotional and painful.

Losing her hair was painfully emotional for Kim. I knew her well enough to tell. But she kept smiling. Why? Kim didn't want others to be uncomfortable with her shaved head. Most women don't choose to shave their head. A woman's clothing can hide her altered chest. People don't see the chemical war raging inside. But everyone sees a woman's hair. When it's missing, people notice.

I learned something about my wife that day when all of her hair hit the floor. I thought that I knew her pretty well. We had dated for six years, and at the time of her diagnosis, we'd been married twenty-three years. Not until her hair was on the floor did I know that she had a birthmark on the back of her head.

After the shaving, I called her mom to let her know about the dreaded deed. I asked her, "Did you know that Kim has a birthmark?" Of course, her mom knew the exact location.

For me, seeing Kim's shaved head was alarming. When a person radically changes their appearance—whether by choice or necessity—it's natural to take a second look if not to just flat out stare. Call it the shock factor. The reaction is understandable.

I tried to act as if her shaved head was no big deal. If temporarily losing her hair was a residual effect of beating cancer, then so be it. Kim also tried to be as nonchalant as possible. Certainly, she cared and it was traumatic. But she had two boys to worry about, ages thirteen and seventeen. Kim didn't want to create any discomfort for them. During the next few hair-free months, she was intentional not to let our oldest son see her without at least a scarf on her head because she was sure that he was very uncomfortable with all that was happening.

Seventeen-year-old boys have their minds on things other than their sick mother. Jim and his buddies had their first vehicles, mostly four-wheel drive jeeps and trucks, and there were off-road mud trails that desperately needed exploration. Four wheeling is much more fun than cancer.

Our oldest son, Jim, was rarely intentional about tending to Kim. Part of that was his personality, and part of that was his understanding of what was happening with his mother. He was always sweet to her when he was home. Years later, he admitted that he failed to understand the severity of his mom's health challenge.

On more than one occasion, I needed to stay with Kim at a time that she needed something from the pharmacy. I once called my son, who was off-roading, and asked him to go pickup the drugs. He balked, as the timing was inconvenient while he was deep in the woods. "Son, this is not an option. Your family needs you, and we need you now," I said.

He ran the errand to the pharmacy.

On yet other occasions, I told him to go to his mother's bedside, sit in the chair next to her, and talk. That level of attention did not come naturally for him. But he did visit with her, showing gentleness and kindness. The exercise did not hurt him one bit. I feel that his time with his mom probably reduced his fears and grew his understanding.

Our youngest son, Jacob, was four years younger. He didn't have the independence of his older brother. Jacob was stuck at home more. And on multiple occasions, he accompanied us to a chemotherapy treatment or follow-up appointments. Both then and as a young man, Jacob shows much empathy for others. He's the go-to guy for peer counseling. He likes solving problems and helping people. During the first chemo treatments, he was home because school was out for the summer. Being with Kim to offer encouragement and assistance was more natural for him.

I have little doubt that if Jacob had his driver's license at the time of Kim's illness, he also would have been gone more often. He had many friends, and for Millenials, friends often matter more than family. I was fortunate to have his assistance.

Parents facing a catastrophic health issue shouldn't shield their children from the truth. How the family processes their challenges will depend on the age and personality of the child. Never lie to your child, particularly about life-and-death issues.

Following the shave, the cancer journey entered a completely new phase—scarves and wigs. The scarves were fun with all of their colors and styles. Kim's friends enjoyed giving those to her. Eventually, she would need a wig. We needed several tries to get one that worked for her. When we landed on a style and color, she wore the wig well and received many compliments. The style was different from any she had ever had, and it caught the attention of many people. She probably got more compliments on her wig—particularly from strangers—than any other hairstyle she had chosen. Strangers would approach her and ask where she got her hair done. Kim's response reflected her concern for others. First, she didn't want to embarrass them, or second, make them feel uncomfortable. So she would quietly tell them it was a wig, and often didn't even mention the cancer.

After her diagnosis in March, Kim's last intravenous chemo treatment was in November. There would be some oral chemo regimens and some ongoing cosmetic surgery. Kim would continue to see her oncologist regularly. By all accounts, the cancer went away. Still, the questions lingered.

Why Kim? Why now? What were we supposed to learn from this? What good could possibly come from this illness?

A cancer diagnosis gives a person much time to think. Unlike a heart attack when a person is "one and done," a cancer patient can wrestle with the big questions of life. In the infusion room during chemo treatments, we heard patients philosophizing with all sorts of rhetoric. Frankly, much of it was secular or humanistic. Our approach was different. If you want big answers, you need a big teacher. You can't get much bigger than your Creator.

We attacked cancer on two levels. First, there was ground zero where we worked the problem. With focus and commitment, we became foot soldiers practicing hand-to-hand combat with the enemy. When your health or even your life is at risk, focusing on wellness consumes you. Still, there are some quiet moments in the foxhole to look at the heavens and wonder, which leads to the second level of attack—spiritual. Nothing forces one to ponder the eternal more than when they face their mortality.

I wanted answers as much as anyone would in that situation. The search for answers took me to Scripture where I developed a theology of healing that asks the ancient question of why bad things happen to good people. That study and the outcomes are in Part Two.

One outcome that we wanted to draw was this: surely, lightning wouldn't strike twice. "Okay, Lord. We faced this one and You gave us victory. We won't have to go through anything like this again, will we?"

Chapter Three

Thunder in the Distance

IN 2012, I BEGAN occasionally to walk awkwardly. My right foot would randomly land squarely on the ground instead of the normal heal-to-toe cadence. I noticed it, as did Kim. As usual, we joked about it as we both claimed I was walking like a horse because the sound resembled a hoof squarely striking the ground.

My suspicion was that my spine or hips were out of alignment, which had often been a problem for me. The solution was typically simple, either some anti-inflammatory drugs or chiropractic adjustments seemed to fix those problems.

On a routine visit to my general practitioner in early 2012, I had a list of questions to discuss. I was 56 at the time, and my body was showing normal signs of wear and tear. My new walking cadence was on the list.

The doctor called it drop foot. Fine, now we have a diagnosis. What does it mean? He asked if I'd be willing to see a neurologist.

Why not? I had plenty of time because I was "self-employed" and entering my second year without full-time employment. A business I had started was hardly thriving, and I was frustrated beyond measure. So yes, I had time but more than that, I was curious about what was happening with me physically.

Back in January 2010, I was awaiting a delayed flight departure from Hartsfield-Jackson International Airport. After sitting for nearly four hours, someone near me dropped a cell phone. I instinctively bent over to pick it up for them and pulled something in my lower back. That led to excruciating pain over the next few months that often made walking difficult. Not only was I uncomfortable, but I was also concerned about my oldest son's upcoming wedding in April. Jim and his fiancé, Jadie, had asked me to officiate. That appointment was not one I intended to miss. Through a series of adjustments, steroid injections, and some physical therapy, the pain eventually subsided from what appeared to be a compression. I regained full mobility, performed the wedding, and life was good. So when I visited a neighborhood neurologist two years later, I fully expected them to pick up that trail. They would confirm the compression issue, make a recommendation—exercise and anti-inflammatory drugs—and all would be well.

The neurologists ordered MRI and CAT scans that failed to confirm a serious compression. Because I was weak on the right side from the hip down, they assumed strengthening would help, so I started physical therapy. The foot drop raised concerns about falls, which I had experienced. Mostly, I blamed the falls on weak ankles and poor footing. Eventually, they ordered an electromyogram (EMG) nerve-conduction study. This exciting procedure involves probing the patient's skin with needles before sending electrical shocks down the nerve. The machine then measures the nerve's ability to carry the electrical current, thus indicating the health of the nerve.

"Hhhmm!"

That response is not one a patient wants to hear during an EMG.

"What's the problem?" I asked.

"The nerve isn't connected to the muscle," the neurologist said.

I imagined a lamp cord unplugged from a wall socket.

Doctors don't like being stumped, but clearly this specialist was bumfuzzled. A score of possibilities were racing through his head because the EMG was not definitive. That test simply recognized the symptom, not the cause. He had no diagnosis. Keep doing physical therapy, he said.

Several months later, the neurologists requested some blood tests. Another clue emerged. Two enzymes—creatine kinase and aldolase—showed high elevations. These elevated enzymes indicate muscle breakdown, but don't explain why.

This medical journey was clearly a needle-in-the-haystack search. Each step created a clue, but no definitive answer. The neurologists were somewhat coy, probably to reduce my alarm. No panic. Let's keep searching.

New career opportunity

During this time, I felt fine. Many good things were happening in my life. In December 2012, I had my first face-to-face job interview for a full-time position, and it came two years after my "voluntary retirement." My income had fallen about 80 percent during those two years. We had scraped the bottom of the barrel, and we needed a breakthrough. This job appeared to be the answer.

Precept Ministries International of Chattanooga had an opening for someone to travel internationally and establish volunteer networks in support of local inductive Bible studies. I was familiar with this ministry and had practiced the inductive method of Bible study since college. Precept is the champion of this study method as led by its co-founder, Kay Arthur. Precept received more than 150 resumes for the position. They chose me and one other person.

The job was a good fit and very similar to what I had done for twenty-five years. This opportunity was a match. Kim and I were ready and willing to make the move to Chattanooga and start a new life. Given the somewhat nonchalant approach of the neurologists, my relative good health, and the promise of a new opportunity, we could not imagine that anything would get in the way of this move.

In December 2012, my general practitioner recommended that I have a muscle biopsy. That is an outpatient procedure whereby a general surgeon makes about a four-inch incision near your hip and removes a section of muscle. The neurologists weren't so quick to pull the trigger until I pressed them for a follow-up blood test to recheck the enzyme levels. We had started this exploration process, and I wanted an answer before moving my family. If this condition reoccurred after the move, we would be dealing with a new set of doctors in a new city. The new job wouldn't start until February, so I had plenty of time. I was anxious to prove that this was no big deal.

The second blood test confirmed the elevated enzymes, so the neurologists ordered the muscle biopsy. Having minor surgery didn't concern me. I wanted an answer to confirm our decision to move. We were going to Chattanooga. God had thrown open a huge door of opportunity at just the right time. We were so sure of this decision that the medical testing seemed like a sideshow.

On January 26, our children joined us and helped load a portable container. We needed to start getting our house ready for sale. Besides all the stuff we began to throw away and donate, we put six tons of stuff in that container. Next stop, Chattanooga.

On January 27, I resigned my position as pastor of Sugarloaf International Fellowship (SIF). This was a part-time position that had begun in July 2011 and had become the center of my vocational universe. The congregation was Korean-American, consisting mostly of college students. More than they needed me, I needed them. When a person feels called to vocational ministry and their ministry gets stripped away, the void is deep. To be what God called me to be, I needed engagement in a tangible ministry.

Following retirement, I applied for scores of pastorates with Anglo churches. I finished seminary in December 1985 and by February 1986, I was working for a mission agency as a magazine and curriculum editor. During 25 years with that agency, I performed most of the functions of a pastor even if only on a temporary basis. But I had never officially held the title of pastor. So I learned that at my age, if you've not been a pastor you can't be a pastor. No one was interested in someone my age with no apparent pastoral experience.

The Koreans took a chance on a middle-aged Anglo who had never been a pastor. Kim and I loved this congregation. The church grew numerically and spiritually. My time at SIF proved to be one of the most satisfying periods of my life. But it was a part-time position with a small salary, and the church knew I needed full-time employment. I applied for many jobs in Atlanta for which I was qualified. There was rarely a call back, much less an interview or offer.

The congregation knew that my tenure would probably be brief. At that point, I had been with them about 19 months. I could only pray that they would understand.

A new plan

On January 28, I had a follow-up appointment with the neighborhood neurologist to get the pathology report on the muscle biopsy. On that Monday morning, Kim and I walked into a discombobulated practice. One of the two neurologists was sick, patients were streaming into the waiting room, and they didn't have my pathology report.

In the examination room, the doctor was clearly uncomfortable, presumably because he didn't have the information we needed. He left the room and made calls to the surgeon and to Emory, a leading medical center in Atlanta, where another neurologist had examined the biopsy. Upon rejoining us in the examination room, the neurologist didn't look upbeat. He didn't want to tell us what we didn't want to hear.

The initial diagnosis was progressive muscular atrophy (PMA), which is preliminary to amyotrophic lateral sclerosis (ALS), or Lou Gehrig's disease. Suddenly, instead of talking about world travel and fulfilling careers, I learned that I had five to ten years to live.

A terminal diagnosis was the last thing we expected. Kim and I were so sure that God was leading us to Chattanooga that this scenario was incomprehensible. My mother lived until she was 76; my father was alive and remarkably healthy in his mid 80s. Maybe there was a mistake.

We needed a second opinion. Emory has an ALS Center. But you don't call them; they call you for an appointment. My neighborhood neurologist recommended me to Emory, and we waited for the call.

The initial diagnosis came exactly one week before starting the new position in Chattanooga. On Wednesday, January 30, I made the uncomfortable call to Precept to inform them that I had to decline the job. Several friends had recommended that I start work in Chattanooga as we couldn't be sure how soon this disease might play out. Precept's financial offer had matched my previous salary. This job was the career and financial solution that we had prayed about for two years. Having spent twenty-five years in a similar ministry, I knew how precious ministry dollars could be. Deception and fraud are not my modus operandi. The right thing to do was to allow Precept to free up that position and seek another candidate.

On Thursday, January 31, Kim and I were in the same den with our sons and daughter-in-law where we had announced Kim's cancer diagnosis to our boys eleven years earlier. Getting five busy adults together on a weeknight is no small task. But each adjusted their schedule to attend a family meeting. We don't do this often; they knew something was up.

As both a journalist and a pastor, I've been trained to tell the truth and let the people decide. Don't hide or sugarcoat truth. Just state the facts. The fact was that lightning had struck twice in our family. I had received a terminal diagnosis, and we wouldn't be moving to Chattanooga.

Our kids are strong and smart. They immediately asked a score of what-if questions. Each showed interest in a solution, though none of us understood how medically elusive that solution might be.

As we awaited the second opinion from Emory, one thing was sure. We still had to move. Our home had two flights of stairs and sat on one-third of an acre. I could no longer walk the stairs or maintain the lawn.

Having six-tons already loaded in a container was just the first step. With spring approaching, we hustled to get the property ready for a hungry market, as housing inventories were low in our area. The stairs were becoming more difficult for me to use. Exhausting fatigue slowed me down further.

The objectives seemed obvious—move into a ranch-style house that would be wheelchair accessible. But for me, there was a second objective. We needed a house that would work for Kim long term. The floor plan had to work for her regardless of my health diagnosis.

Meanwhile, we didn't broadcast the news yet. Emory did call and set an appointment for February 19, 2013. In just a few weeks, we would have a second opinion from a clinic that specializes in ALS. So we held onto hope in the midst of much prayer that the second opinion would bring different news. Nothing felt official until we got the second opinion.

Kim and I are from Kentucky, and our families there knew that I was supposed to start a new job. They had a right to know that I would not be starting that job. So on Super Bowl Sunday 2013, I called both of our surviving parents, my mother-in-law and my father. The news saddened my mother in law, and she offered encouragement. My father went silent. The news shocked him so much that he hardly responded. He was alone in Kentucky, and I hated ending that call.

A catastrophic diagnosis affects different people in different ways. For some, a diagnosis creates stress that manifests in any number of unpredictable ways. We didn't know for another month that my father woke up the next morning with Bells Palsy, which typically is short-term facial paralysis. The paralysis soon dissipated, and his face was normal.

One person's illness is not isolated. Just as with cancer, there's one patient but a host of victims.

Chapter Four

Lightning Strikes

AMYOTROPHIC LATERAL SCLEROSIS is not a common disease. Not many doctors specialize in ALS, and most are unfamiliar with the few available drugs. First identified in 1869, the diagnosis of New York Yankee legend Lou Gehrig with ALS in the late 1930s thrust the disease into the limelight. Perhaps as much as any ALS patient, Gehrig represents both the irony and cruelty of the disease. He was the "Iron Horse" of baseball, having played fourteen seasons with the Bronx Bombers and appearing in 2,130 consecutive games. His last game was April 30, 1939. Gehrig died on June 2, 1941, at age thirty-seven.

I'm a lifelong baseball fan and had read about Gehrig and his contemporary, Babe Ruth. These men led a Yankees' team that dominated baseball during their era and became legendary. On July 4, 1939, when the Yankees retired Gehrig's number and honored him in a ceremony at Yankee Stadium, he made one of the most poignant statements in sports history, "Fans, for the past two weeks you have been reading about the bad break I got. Yet today I consider myself the luckiest man on the face of the earth."

On February 19, 2013, I also considered myself lucky to be living in a major city with one of the few ALS research centers in the nation. The Emory ALS Center is a leader in experimental treatments, including stem-cell research. If we could get a definitive answer or learn of a possible cure, we would likely discover it there.

ALS is a guilt-free disease. You can't eat, smoke, drink, or philander yourself into this illness. Only 10-15 percent of ALS patients inherit the disease genetically. Based upon current knowledge, ALS strikes randomly, mostly among males. There's no known cause and no known cure, though researchers always seem to be on the doorstep of a major breakthrough. Currently, ALS is a maintenance disease as health-care providers attend to a patient until death.

At Emory, two resident physicians thoroughly examined me before I met with the director. The final word would come from him.

"It's ALS. I don't know how else to tell you. It's straight up ALS," he said.

Imagine for a moment that in your profession, you regularly meet strangers and inform them about a terminal diagnosis. The doctors are as human as the patient in the room is. They don't know how a patient might react to the news. Will the patient cry, scream, and yell? Will the patient faint? Will the patient become angry and demanding? This team of three doctors braced for our response. I could tell they were uncomfortable.

"There's something you need to now," I calmly told them. "This is the third time I've had this conversation. My mother had Alzheimer's disease and my wife is a breast cancer survivor. Just tell us what we're dealing with here."

The standard prognosis is that ALS patients live three to five years from onset. The question then becomes, when did the disease begin to manifest? Clearly, I was showing symptoms in the winter and spring of 2012. Based upon my medical history, the Emory team's conclusion was that I'd been sick since 2010.

ALS progresses at a steady rate, but the rate varies among

patients. Some die within three years; some patients live for decades. Based upon their conclusion that I was two years into the disease and still walking without aids, the doctors figured that my progression was relatively slow.

Before our visit ended, we had met with scores of nurses, advocates, and specialists who create a clinical ALS team. Kim's breast cancer diagnosis had thrust her into a rather large sorority. Women with breast cancer are like sisters. Their common experience creates immediate identity. They've been there, and done that. Our visit to Emory was akin to a fraternal initiation. You're in; you're one of us. This is how we do life.

News of a mentor

During all the activity, there was a short break in the action. I checked my email and learned that a mentor had died. Don Rutledge was an acclaimed globetrotting photojournalist who had lived an extraordinary life. As a young man, he had documented John Howard Griffin's transition from being white to black in 1959. Griffin wanted to experience what life was like for blacks in the South. Don received very little recognition or credit for his photography on that project, which validated Griffin's transition and catapulted his memoir, *Black Like Me*, onto the national stage. Don eventually documented Christian missions around the world. At the time we met, I was a photojournalism student at Western Kentucky University. Don had encouraged me and became a role model for how photography could be a ministry that spoke loudly and broadly to inform and encourage engagement in Christian missions. Besides being a Blackstar agency photographer, Don was a seminary-trained, ordained minister who felt that he communicated better via photography than from a pulpit. Cameras were his platform.

Don had been sick for years since retiring, so his death was no surprise. As I read the obituary, I had peace. Though Don had been quite frail, he was okay now. I had no doubt that God honored Don's faithfulness. Yes, my friend and mentor was okay, and I would be, too.

As I was learning of Don's death, Kim asked a question while we were still alone.

"I wonder what made the doctors conclude that it's ALS. What one thing caused them to draw that conclusion?"

We asked to see the lead doctor again, and he soon rejoined us. Kim posed her question, and the doctor's answer was this: "I know it when I see it." He had read the pathology and other lab reports, but seeing me walk and do the strength tests must have contributed to his diagnosis. This team of experts had committed their lives to ALS research and treatment; it's their world. He showed no hesitancy. This man was convinced.

Clearly, this news isn't what we wanted to hear. Our hope was similar to the early stages of cancer when we held out hope that there would been some diagnostic mistake and all evidence of the disease had disappeared. The few that knew about the diagnosis at this point were praying with us for a miracle. The miracle wasn't shaping up the way we had envisioned.

Our visit enveloped us with information. Just like with cancer, ALS thrust us into a world that we would rather not have visited. ALS was our new reality. This disease would claim my life about thirty years sooner than I had anticipated dying. But I wasn't dead yet. There was still time to live and much to accomplish.

Early on, I made an important decision. I would not be in denial about ALS, but I would also not surrender to the disease. I would continue to be as productive as possible for as long as possible. I would laugh and love, and I would enjoy family and friends. Life wasn't over yet.

When problems arise in our marriage, Kim and I knuckle down and work the problem. We look for solutions, and we needed many.

We still needed to downsize into a new home. I'd just turned down a full-time job because of the diagnosis, so we had income challenges. "Okay, God. We need you to show up and to show up big."

Time to tell

I stayed composed until the following Sunday. The day before receiving the initial diagnosis in late January, I had resigned as pastor of Sugarloaf International Fellowship (SIF) in Suwanee, Georgia. Because we fully anticipated that I would be starting a new full-time job in about eight days, it was time to let them know. I would be commuting home on weekends for several months, so I could continue to preach on Sundays. This transition wouldn't happen fast.

Following the second opinion, I knew emphatically that we'd not be moving to Chattanooga for the new job. The church leadership was aware of my diagnosis and had asked me to stay as long as I could, which I agreed to do. Still, the congregation needed an explanation. I had resigned several weeks before; now I was staying. We had a definitive diagnosis. There was nothing to hide.

At the end of what appeared to be a normal service, I did the typical announcements and the congregation prepared for dismissal. That's when I told them there was one more announcement.

Just as we had done with our family, my goal was to simply state the facts. No embellishment; no sugarcoating. So I reminded them about the resignation a few weeks earlier, but there had been some changes. I told them about the ALS diagnosis. Hardly anyone in the congregation understood the diagnosis. They were grabbing their smart phones to Google the disease. My goal wasn't to give them a clinical explanation of ALS; I simply wanted them to know that I was facing a health challenge.

All of that went fine until I made the mistake of trying to explain how much I loved this congregation. Good-bye composure.

Scripture defines a pastor as being like a shepherd who cares for his flock. A congregation is under the watch care of a pastor. He feels much responsibility for them, loves them, and tries to disciple them. Kim and I had grown to love deeply the people of this congregation. SIF was such an unusual situation as a Korean-American congregation of mostly collegiates had invited a middle-aged Anglo—who had never held the title of pastor—to be their shepherd. God had blessed this unusual union, and I loved being their pastor.

The congregation soon surrounded and prayed over Kim and me. I feel sure that many didn't understand that I had just informed them that my diagnosis was terminal. But they were there for us on that day. Even as they physically surrounded us, scores of others would do the same spiritually and emotionally. Kim and I were about to learn again about the power of faith and friendships.

Chapter Five

Good Medicine

RECEIVING A TERMINAL DIAGNOSIS for a disease with an unknown cause or cure gets one's attention. Unlike cancer, which has warehouses full of drugs, my physicians offered me just one. The good news was that unlike chemotherapy drugs, this drug had virtually no side effects, they said. No nausea. No hair loss. Just take it twice a day. Studies show that patients taking this particular drug live longer than those who don't. So I began taking the drug.

During Kim's cancer treatments, we were visiting doctors at least once a week. Cancer is a very hands-on treatment. ALS is less so. The regimen was to visit the ALS center every four to six months, allow them to measure the disease's progression, ask questions, and make decisions about the subsequent steps of managing the disease.

During the next months, we held out much hope that the experimental treatments would work for me. If nothing else, whether the treatments worked or not, I wanted to be part of the solution as researchers continue to unravel the mystery of ALS. Though ALS stem-cell treatment was new and unproven, I was willing to participate.

One summer afternoon, I received a call from a friend who had just returned from medical treatments in Asia where she had sought help for a different malady. While there, she learned that Korea was within two years of stem-cell treatments for ALS, but Japan and China were already offering treatments. "Sell everything you have and go to Asia now," my friend strongly advised.

After the telephone conversation, I stepped into our den where Kim was listening to a local television story. Stem-cell treatments at Emory had reportedly cured a man with ALS.

The next morning I was communicating with Emory to verify what we heard and to ask, perhaps selfishly, what about me? If the clinic I attended was discovering critical breakthroughs, surely I could participate.

By September, we'd settled the issue. First, the experimental study with stem cells was only for patients whose diagnosis came less than two years ago. The conclusion was that I'd been sick more than two years. Second, the stem cell application happens surgically through the neck. Neurosurgeons expose the spinal cord and inject stem cells there. In 2004, I had cervical surgery that resulted in a fusion and the insertion of a cadaver disk. The surgery was successful as it relieved much pain, but it also eliminated me from stem-cell consideration. I represented more risk than did other patients. Third, the stem-cell source was a fetus. Learning that a medical facility founded by a major protestant denomination was practicing fetal stem-cell treatments surprised us. Further, that information presented a moral question for us. Neither Kim nor I support abortion, and we don't believe in sacrificing a person—particular when that person has no voice—to prolong life for someone like me. Other stem cell sources exist, and we believe the research should focus there.

We also learned that the Emory team wasn't sure why the man on television showed recovery from ALS. After applied, stem cells take much time to cause any positive result. This man's response had been almost immediate, leaving the team to decide whether the healing came from his pre-operative regimen. So there was good news, but science still couldn't yield an explanation. Sometimes, answers just lead to more questions.

Desire for healing

Within eight months of receiving the ALS diagnosis, Kim and I had come to understand that modern medicine could offer us much support, but little hope. If I were to experience healing, the source would be nonmedical. So I had a little talk with Jesus, reminding Him about the resurrection of Lazarus, Jairus' daughter, and the widow's son at Nain. Compared to a resurrection, healing an ALS patient should be simple. Then I volunteered for a miracle. Throughout the New Testament, Jesus performed miracles to prove the power of God. The miracles also proved that Jesus was God incarnate. (See more on this in Part Two.)

I wanted to experience God's miraculous healing power. Clearly, my motives were somewhat selfish. When a man has a loving family, rewarding work, and good friends, he has much to live for. Yes, I wanted to live. But I also wanted a story of healing to encourage others.

Just as with Kim's cancer, we not only faced a physical challenge, but we also faced a faith challenge. How much could we trust God through the ALS journey?

Shortly after the diagnosis, we had to make some big decisions. Among those was whether to apply for disability. On the day of my second opinion at Emory, the staff handed me a signed letter proclaiming me disabled. They advised me to contact Social Security, which I did that day. The conversation with the Social Security customer service agent that day was more upsetting than the confirmation of a terminal diagnosis. In my lifetime, my employers and I had paid more than $200,000 into Social Security. Now, I was going to have to jump through major hoops, and eventually receive about a quarter of the monthly income I had earned before my "voluntary retirement." Plus, my income had to be only about $1,040 per month before I could apply, and then there would be a six-month waiting period before receiving the first disability check. Whatever happened to government for the people?

Somehow, someway, I could have milked the system right away. Apparently, people do this all the time. Perhaps it was pride, but I didn't want to submit to federal inspection of my health and finances any sooner than necessary. Besides, I had some writing contracts that were challenging and motivating, and I was enjoying my part-time role as pastor. I would rather work than await subvention. I prefer independence, not dependence.

The disease slowly created new realities that changed my capacity to perform routine functions. For me, fatigue was one of the first signs. The summer before receiving the diagnosis, I could barely mow my yard. Our home was on one-third-acre of land. Instead of trying to mow the entire yard in one day, I'd do it in two. Each time I blamed my stamina on being out of shape and needing to get to the gym. But we had been living on an 80 percent drop in income, so gym memberships weren't in the budget.

After the diagnosis, I noticed the fatigue issues more. I remained independent, but I was learning to calculate my outings and exertion. No longer could I just casually go to the grocery store. Now, I was more aware of how much walking one does there. Walking increased my risk of stumbling, as unexpectedly, a foot would drag, particularly when I had been walking a while. Life was changing, and I needed to make adjustments and swallow some pride.

The time had come to enter the blue zone.

Swallowing my pride

Applying for a handicapped parking permit is not a difficult process in Georgia. I already had a letter of declaration about my disability.

My goal was to remain as independent as possible for as long as possible. Achieving that goal would require adjustments.

Like many people, I've had more than my fair share of skepticism about the people parking in the blue zone. Few look disabled; most just appear to be in a hurry.

Apparently, others share my skepticism. The view *from* the blue zone is different from the view *into* the blue zone. Many people watch you. Mostly they glance, but the experience begins to feel somewhat like a zoo animal on display. Perhaps people are curious to know if your permit is legitimate. Perhaps as citizen police, they desire to see verification of your malady. Most likely, they're just nosy.

Living in the blue zone represents one of the many big gulps of pride one must swallow with ALS. Another gulp came after a dangerous and public embarrassment.

A neighboring church asked me to speak at a singles event. This church's niche was among young Korean-American single professionals. These young adults had begun their careers and were ready to marry. But, first things first, they needed to find a suitable mate. My goal was to encourage them in part by sharing our story.

Kim and I were high-school sweethearts. We started dating at ages seventeen and fifteen. Six years later, we married. Our relationship was typical of small-town America in the early 1970s. We had a strong sense of community. Each came from stable families. Kim's family owned one of the few entertainment businesses in town, a bowling center. My father was a civil engineer employed by the state. We had scores of friends and big dreams. But none of those dreams included cancer or ALS.

On our wedding day in 1979, we made a covenant of loyalty in sickness and in health. Even when everyone is *healthy*, marriage is challenging. By the time Kim learned she had breast cancer, we had already navigated graduate school, career changes, cross-country moves, and having children. *Healthy* was plenty challenging.

Wedding days are a blur to the bride and groom. The couple is nervous and excited, the center of everyone's attention. So when the time comes to make those vows, are they sincere or just mouthing words?

What I certainly didn't realize on my wedding day was that I was standing next to the one person on this globe that I would trust with my end-of-life decisions. I have full confidence in her to make those decisions. She knows my desires, and she loves me. She will do what's best for the family and for me.

How many brides and grooms do you know who think that way on or before their wedding day? In effect, that's one of the statements you're making in a wedding ceremony. If more brides and grooms understood that, maybe they would be more judicious concerning the person with whom they walk down the aisle.

I had poured out my heart that night to the Korean-American young professionals. My challenge was to be wise as they date and to look hard at the character of potential marriage partners. Could you trust that person with your end-of-life decisions?

Then I closed the presentation with prayer, took a step back, stumbled, and fell flat on my back. Talk about a downer. That's not the recommended finish to public speaking.

Fortunately, I was not hurt. My embarrassment made up for any hurt.

This happened about a month before my scheduled graduation from a doctoral studies program. The seminary issuing the degree is growing, and there would be a large crowd there. My family would be traveling together for the occasion. Making a scene at my graduation was not something I desired.

So I bought a cane. Doing so was the first public admission that something was wrong. The cane started to trigger some questions, but interestingly, most people appeared to be afraid to ask. Using the cane was awkward at first, and I was very self-conscious. But after it prevented a few falls, it was time to bury my ego. The cane wasn't shame; it was freedom. A simple walking stick was prolonging my independence.

At my doctoral graduation, there were scores of graduate students receiving degrees. I was the only one using a cane. With some assistance, I navigated the steps, received my degree, and managed to avoid a scene.

That's a good day.

The good news is that there have been many good days since the ALS diagnosis. One of the best was the day I received a phone call from Precept, the ministry I had planned to join full time.

"We believe that God led us to you for a reason, and we'd still like to work with you," said the representative. "Will you come to Chattanooga so that we can talk further?"

I'd spent twenty-five years in a ministry that forced "voluntary retirement" as I reached senior adulthood. Now, here was another ministry for which I had not worked a day that was exhibiting extraordinary integrity. We soon negotiated a contract agreement that allowed me to work primarily from home with some travel to Chattanooga. The work didn't just help us financially, but it gave me a strong sense of purpose and worth. That's a good day.

We were able to sell our home in three days due to a low-housing inventory in our area. While selling in that environment worked in our favor, finding a new home proved more challenging. Patience and persistence worked as we eventually were able to find a house that met our needs, aligned with the closing of our residence, and was less expensive than the home we had sold. Family and friends volunteered unselfishly to help us on both sides of the move. The day we moved in, there were 40 volunteers at our new house. That's a hectic day, but a good day.

Friends and family continued to overwhelm us with acts of kindness, both big and small. Sometimes the gift was tangible; often it was just a gesture of concern or help. On more than one occasion, that help came from strangers.

During a stop for gas, I fell in a convenience store bathroom. I don't know if you've ever found yourself sitting helplessly on a public bathroom floor, but it's not pleasant. At that point, I no longer had the ability to pick myself up. So what do you do? Cry? Honestly, what good would that have done? Call 911? That seemed like over kill. Call a family member? No one was close. There only seemed to be one option: Mr. Self Sufficient would push the door open with his cane, scoot out to the floor of the convenience store, and ask the attendant for help.

A woman was running the store that day. She was calm and understood my predicament when I explained why I couldn't get up. I figured that I needed at least two men to help. "Were there any around?" I asked. "No, but one might be here soon," she said. So we waited.

The next adult male to enter the store was apparently a customer. She asked him to help, and the man immediately came to my aid. He said the right things and did the right things. Instead of waiting for another male, this stranger and the woman attendant each grabbed an arm and lifted me up. With me pushing some, I was soon upright and stable.

What I remember most about that random encounter was how gentle each person was. They were sympathetic and understanding. They didn't panic or ask many questions. Despite the fall, that was a good day.

God continually met needs through people like the two strangers at the convenience store. Acts of kindness made up for the lack of medical solutions. Those actions became the best medicine available to me. Knowing that people cared and having positive interaction with others made for good days.

Chapter Six

Making Adjustments

THE DAY OUR NEIGHBORHOOD neurologist said that I had a terminal disease, my thoughts were about Kim. The diagnosis caught us by surprise, but I knew enough about ALS to realize that this wasn't going to be easy. ALS is a high-maintenance disease requiring much care in the later stages. Kim would take responsibility for my care, and given her natural desire to serve and please others, I knew this challenge could consume her. That responsibility isn't what I wanted for my wife.

Like most couples in their mid fifties, we were looking forward to retirement, grandkids, travel, and maybe even new career challenges. The golden years had been looking good. Now we were making an unexpected sharp turn onto a path we hadn't chosen. How we navigated this new path with its unfamiliarity, potholes, obstructions, and unwelcome destiny would determine the quality of our relationship henceforth. My determination was to make this as painless as possible for Kim, the person I love the most.

With a terminal diagnosis, a family must make scores of decisions—both big and small. Whom do we tell and how do we tell people about the diagnosis? Do we move and if so, where do we move? Do we stay in Atlanta or return to our home in Kentucky? How do I navigate two flights of stairs? What about driving? What about applying for disability?

The decision-making required something well beyond our human capacity. We needed supernatural wisdom and discernment. There were too many variables; too many possibilities. We needed help making wise decisions.

The diagnosis created a health crisis, but not a crisis of faith or belief. Unlike most families that receive a catastrophic health diagnosis, we had faced this before when Kim had breast cancer. I had struggled as a husband and a minister with the big questions about death and dying, healing and prayer. Those questions are overwhelming, sometimes confusing, and consume much energy. (You will find help with those questions in Part Two.)

The greatest resource we had for this journey was our faith in God. I'd spent more than twenty-five years in vocational ministry traveling the world to tell people that God was loving, caring, saving, and powerful. And I believed that with all my heart. This challenge gave me the option to practice what I had preached.

For me, the issue is rather black and white. Either God is real, or He's not. Either Jesus is God incarnate who brought salvation to mankind, or He's a liar. The faith that I claimed was either real or fabricated, and therefore false.

One of the first decisions one must make is whether they'll be mad at God. Anger is a natural outcome when you or a loved one faces a catastrophic health diagnosis. Here's the good news. God's big enough to handle your anger, and He's patient and loving. Be angry for only a moment, and then move on. Fueling your anger can lead to bitterness, and what healing are you likely to find in bitterness? I had too much to be thankful for to allow bitterness to define me. God has blessed me with purpose. He has given me a wonderful family. He has allowed us to travel and experience more of the world than most people will ever see. Because of that, regret did not fill my soul. Instead, thankfulness filled that void and gave me the freedom to focus on pressing issues.

New home

Clearly, we had to make decisions that helped us manage my health care. That reality was a given, though the attention was uncomfortable for me. My determination was that we would make decisions that were good for Kim. For instance, we had to move into a ranch-style home that would be wheelchair accessible. But beyond that objective, I didn't want our home to be a hospital. The next home had to be one that Kim could love and likely live in the rest of her life if she so chose. As we looked at properties, I wanted to see that gleam in her eye that said, "Yes, I'd love to make this our home. This house is the one."

When we found that property, it was under contract to another buyer. But there was a deadline for financing. If the buyer didn't qualify by that date, we could be next in line. So we kept looking. This was a wonderful home with a unique and inviting floor plan. Surely, the original buyer would qualify.

Following a long weekend, we learned that the first contract fell through. We moved quickly to sign a new contract, and Kim got her house. Now, we had to move the logistics of moving into high gear.

More than thirty-three years of marriage had produced many wonderful memories, and gobs of stuff. Gosh, did we have stuff? Kim and I both tend to be pack rats. The home we had lived in for sixteen years in Atlanta had a basement that I had finished out with a large storage room. That idea seemed good at the time, but the convenience of that storage space kept us from being more judicious about what we kept and what we discarded. Needless to say, moving felt more like judgment day. Now, we would have to pay a price for all the junk we had been unable to throw away.

Over the next several weeks, I took multiple truckloads of stuff to local non-profits with thrift stores. I showed up so often that the attendants often rolled their eyes upon my arrival. Each week, other stuff that had been valuable and important at one time covered part of our front lawn awaiting the garbage truck. One day, our sanitation company had a substitute driver. He was alone and hacked off to see what we'd left for him. I reassured him that I'd help load the trash, which I was able to do. Soon, that stuff was gone, too.

Setting your garbage out for pickup is nasty and burdensome. The smells coming from the container are hideous. The collection of disheveled stuff, which now qualifies as trash, represented the chaos that seemed to define our life. We create our own clutter in life, and then we wonder why. For me, trash pickup days became like redemption. Setting your trash and junk on the curb is akin to confession. Everybody has something they need to throw away, to release. Taking the junk and trash to the curb is like that admission. When the truck drives away with your curbside confession, there's a huge sense of relief like a burden lifted. Out of sight, gone. Redemption. Now it was time to move on.

Moving brought much emancipation to the Burtons as we changed addresses in April. The new house would be smaller, and there was no basement to hide our stuff. Though we had thrown many things away, we didn't get rid of enough. Moving took two days. We hired a local moving company to handle the furniture and appliances. They maxed out their truck and left us with more stuff to move on our own over the next few weeks. The next day, we tackled the portable container our kids had helped us load back in January. Forty volunteers came to our new home that Saturday. Many were from the Korean church where I was pastor, but about half were people we didn't even know. A Sunday school class from another church had adopted us. Those six tons got off loaded in about thirty minutes.

During those first four months since the diagnosis, God was showing us His mercy primarily through the kindness of others.

Most of those who reached out were friends and church members with whom we had some degree of relationship. Many of those friendships deepened over the following months. I was particularly appreciative of our Korean friends.

They called me pastor

In June of 2011 when God had opened the door for a middle-aged Anglo from Kentucky to pastor a Korean-American congregation of primarily college students, we were naive enough to accept the invitation. Though not unheard of, it was rare. Normally, Anglos who ministered cross culturally had to board a boat or plane, travel afar, learn a language, and immerse themselves in a new culture. I called my tenure with the Koreans "inverted missions" as the mission field had come to us.

North Atlanta has become one of the most culturally diverse regions in the nation. We discovered that within seven miles of our church were an estimated 120,000 internationals. The church was in Gwinnett County, whose public school system had students who spoke more than one-hundred languages.

Ethnic churches typically worship in their native language when they initially form. The pastor and members are usually first generation, recent immigrants. Many arrived here not knowing English. Eventually, many learn enough English to survive. However, their children, sometimes called 1.5ers or second-generation Americans, grow up with one foot in their family's culture and one in their new culture. They naturally become fluently bilingual and learn how to navigate both cultures.

The children of first-generation Americans become more comfortable with American culture and English as they mature. When they're in college and have more freedom to make decisions for themselves, many begin to leave their parent's church. Some do so because their English skills are better than their native language skills.

Others transition because of peer pressure to be American. In Asian cultures, second-generation Americans often grow weary of their native culture's traditional leadership style, which can be very authoritarian. To address those changes, ethnic churches often start an English ministry or EM. The EM remains tethered to the mother church and primarily serves the children of its members.

Sugarloaf Korean Baptist Church (SKBC) was the first Korean Baptist church in Georgia and had started other Korean churches throughout Georgia. This congregation was healthy and thriving primarily as a Korean-speaking congregation. But they needed help with their EM. Following my "voluntary retirement," I started a service business in an attempt to become self-supporting. Getting a job at my age in our economy coming out of twenty-five years of ministry wasn't going to happen. Age and religious discrimination are subtle, but pervasive. I soon discovered that if I was willing to work for free (straight commission), people would hire me. So in my sudden new career, I called on SKBC. I knew the pastor, and I'd worked with his wife in my previous job. In the process of reconnecting, one day he asked me if I'd preach for their English ministry for the month of July 2011. Ethnic churches have trouble finding good English speakers to lead those ministries, and I just thought I was buying them some time until they could find a Korean American. Their EM didn't meet until 1:30 p.m. on Sundays, and I was regularly supply preaching most mornings about thirty-eight miles away. Churches don't pay part-time preachers well, but that was my only steady income. Plus, I was enjoying the role of pastor. So for several months I was a circuit rider, preaching each Sunday at two churches.

My one-month commitment lasted twenty-nine months. Were it not for ALS, I would have gladly stayed longer. Those twenty-nine months became some of the most fulfilling and challenging of my ministry. Because of my age and lack of official pastoral experience, no Anglo church would even consider me for employment. But the Koreans took a chance on me, believed in me, and allowed me to become their pastor.

They also allowed me to push them. During my first leadership meeting, I brought a toy bulldozer. My goal was not to baby sit, I told them. Within weeks, I had assessed that this was a sleepy congregation of mostly students who had come from the SKBC youth group. We had about six married couples who formed the core families. I planned to challenge and push them to become something more substantial than what they'd been without running over or ahead of the congregation.

Through a series of focus groups and demographic studies, the congregation concluded that it was time to think and act differently. Instead of being an EM, this gathering needed to start the slow process of becoming an independent church. I was naive to how difficult that process might be, but we pushed ahead and eventually launched on August 12, 2012, as Sugarloaf International Fellowship: An Intercultural Worship Gathering. That step was significant and uncommon in ethnic churches. Together, we were plowing new ground.

Had I known about my ALS diagnosis, I seriously doubt that I would have tackled the transition. Throughout the summer, we prepared for a launch that included a block party attended by about 300 people. The logistics of that event drained me, but I continued to blame it on my age and being out of shape. At that time, I had no idea that I was sick.

Because this congregation was primarily college students, I was anxious about their response to my illness when I announced it about seventeen months after the church launched. For most, this would be their first time to know someone with a terminal illness. Would they treat me differently? Would they leave the church because of my health challenge?

They didn't freak out. The congregation grew, particularly our college population.

As the congregation grew, it required more time. Though

happening slowly, I was getting weaker. Those two realities drove me to a tough decision in the ALS journey. Once again, I needed to give up something I loved, something that defined who I was. Yet another gulp of pride mixed with new realities.

I knew for several months that I needed to resign. Yes, my health was part of the reason, but the long-term health of the congregation was the paramount issue. To continue the path we had begun, they needed healthy, hands-on leadership.

November 2013 was my last month to serve as a pastor. Resigning my one and only pastorate was bittersweet. So I focused on thankfulness because God had allowed me this privilege, being grateful for the relationships and lessons learned as a pastor. Any sadness I felt at that time was not as much about leaving as it was about not having a place to go. I wanted to start and pastor another church. That wasn't likely to happen now. God would have to redefine how He wanted me to serve Him.

Chapter Seven

Life Lessons

MONEY CAN'T BUY the best education. Life lessons that truly shape us happen around the dinner table, on the playground, and in small groups. As much as we need to read and write, and add and subtract, we also need to know how to get along on good days and bad.

Just as in school when you have to take courses that don't interest you, life will bring some unwanted tests, too. We didn't want to learn about cancer or ALS. We didn't choose these diseases, but we did choose how to respond. Neither one of us wanted a health challenge to define us.

Clearly, a catastrophic health issue is a game changer. That news rocks your world, particularly when the outcome is terminal. Suddenly, the bell has rung and class has started. God still has things to teach those of us with a terminal disease.

Life Lesson Number One

How you react will set the tone for the family and others.

When our boys were very young, I had returned early one Sunday morning from a weekend trip and surprised the family by joining them at church. Afterwards, we went to a local restaurant for lunch. As our food arrived, one of the boys wanted ketchup. Kim took the bottle and began shaking it violently, not realizing that the cap was loose. She shook that bottle several times before noticing that she was slinging ketchup all over me in my tan suit and on our oldest son. The ketchup was in my hair and on my glasses.

Kim gasped and waited for my reaction. I turned toward my oldest son who had also received a healthy dose of the flying ketchup and looked into his eyes. He was petrified. What's daddy going to do? Will he be angry? What will he say to mommy?

In that split second, I sensed God quickly telling me that this was a teachable moment. How I responded would teach him how to respond when similar things happen in his life. I felt something deep inside me saying, don't mess this up.

I broke out laughing. That immediately released the tension around our table—and the table behind us that also received a helping of unwanted ketchup. Maybe my sons would learn that laughter is better than anger when unfortunate or embarrassing things happen.

Many studies have shown how organizations become a reflection of their leader's personality and values. A leader sets the tone.

When you receive a terminal diagnosis, you're the leader. Scores of people—family, friends, and health professionals—will focus on you. They will respond to your needs as you define those needs. If you're bitter and spiteful, you will make the whole journey miserable for everyone. If you're positive and hopeful, that not only makes the journey more bearable but it also allows you to minister to those who are helping you. Your diagnosis can actually empower you to be a blessing to others.

I sensed this early on in both meetings at the two neurological practices. My diagnosis wasn't the first time either doctor had broken bad news to a patient. But in each practice, the doctors appeared to be very uncomfortable. Doctors aren't gods; they're men and women who want to be agents of healing. My visits were no more fun for them than they were for me. There was no reason to cause them undue alarm. So to the best of my ability, I tried to reassure them that we were okay in receiving their diagnosis.

After the second opinion, we began to tell family and close friends. Once again, I just stated the facts, sometimes over the phone and sometimes face to face. Some cried. Others had a look of bewilderment. With each exchange, I sensed that the other person was waiting for my cue.

I'm not sure how many people who receive a terminal diagnosis have already had a mentor who faced a tough illness. I had been a student in the classroom of life, and my wife had been the teacher. She handled her cancer diagnosis with as much grace, kindness, and faith as anyone I had ever known. Kim was a source of inspiration to countless others and to me. She was my role model.

The journey is not without emotion. Both Kim and I had our moments, but typically, those were private. My tears were on my pillow.

We skipped the pity party and focused on working the problem. The answers included changes in residence and transportation. None of these was easy, but that focus kept us looking forward.

Instead of seeing a catastrophic health diagnosis as a curse, I encourage you to see it as empowerment. The remaining time that a person with a terminal diagnosis has may be the most influential days of their life. Use that precious time wisely.

Life Lesson Number Two

Don't play the victim.

The "why" question happens fast. That's one of the first places we go when bad things happen. Fatal car accidents. Disease diagnosis. Heart attacks. Terrorist attacks. Victims abound in this world. Every time I hear of a suicide bombing in the Middle East, I cringe.

Undoubtedly, most of the deceased were at the wrong place at the wrong time when they became victims of evil intent. Very little makes sense to us when life goes askew.

Blame seems to be one of the first responses, and we aim that blame at God as we ask why. However, anytime we ask tough philosophical questions like why bad thing happen to good people, objectively we have to ask the opposite question.

One night during our church's adult small-group Bible study, I was walking them through the content of Part Two of this book, which is a brief theological treatment of the tough questions we all ask on bad days. That discussion helped me to realize how much they were struggling with my diagnosis. They didn't understand why their pastor had ALS.

My response was, why not? The assumption is that no one deserves maladies, particularly people whom we label as "good." By most accounts, I'm a good guy. I pay my taxes. I don't beat my wife. I don't engage in self-destructive behavior like smoking. But still, I'm a sinner, just like a terrorist or a drunk driver. Though I would never consider or engage in intentional behavior to hurt people, my sin stands in the way of God establishing His holiness in me.

So why do bad things happen to good people? Because good people do bad things. On some level in some way we all lie, cheat, deceive, and hide evil intent in our heart. We hide it from one another, but we can't hide it from God.

Scripture answers this question from its earliest pages. When sin entered the world through the Garden of Eden, it infected each of us. Sin separates us from a holy God, no matter how we measure the severity of our sin.

Consequently, we all must die. Death is the just punishment for our sin. We deserve death. That harsh reality becomes more difficult when in our minds there's no rhyme or reason to an individual—particularly someone close to us—facing major illness or death. The more personal an incident is, the more confusing it can be.

Once we understand that God is still at work even in sickness and death, then our perspective changes. We rarely see the tapestry He's weaving while we're in the storm (see Life Principle 2 in Part Two). So we have an option. We can curse the God of the universe, or we can embrace Him with whatever measure of faith we have. Everything makes more sense in the arms of God.

I chose faith. That choice requires surrender of one's will and full understanding, which is a definition of faith. "Now faith is the assurance of things hoped for, the conviction of things not seen" (Hebrews 11:1). God promises eternity in heaven to those who take Him at His word and accept by faith that Jesus was His incarnate son. I believe that promise. So when I draw my last breath, I have faith that not only will I be in the presence of God, but also that ALS will stay behind in my earthly body. "For our citizenship is in heaven, from which also we eagerly wait for a Savior, the Lord Jesus Christ; who will transform the body of our humble state into conformity with the body of His glory, by the exertion of the power that He has even to subject all things to Himself" (Philippians 2:20-21).

The death of Christians deceives the great deceiver. At the point of death, Satan appears to have won. But one split second later, a Christian is a victor who is receiving his or her just reward, which includes a healed and glorified body.

After the diagnosis, I began personally calling friends and family to tell them about the diagnosis. One person I called was a former youth in a church where I had been a youth leader. She had also worked for me one summer in one of the national ministries for which I was responsible. As we talked, she asked a fair question, "Are you scared?" Her question provoked this thought. Why should a Christ follower be scared of heaven? If Scripture is true, there should be no fear.

So if you're a Christian and become sick, particularly with a terminal diagnosis, avoid the victim mentality. Assume the posture of faith, hope, and great expectation. Death will be your victory (1 Corinthians 14:55).

Life Lesson Number Three

You're now the professor.

In 1996, I started serving as the interim senior adult minister at Germantown Baptist Church near Memphis, Tenn. This was a mega church, and senior adults were the largest population segment, numbering about one thousand.

If you're going to serve as an age-group minister in a local church, work with senior adults. They're the best. They know how to laugh at themselves, and they enjoy one another's company. I spent less than a year in that position, but I learned some valuable life lessons.

One of the senior adults had terminal cancer. Fred Howell was a retired train conductor. He was gregarious, and people loved being around Fred. I found his kind nature to be evident even when I visited Fred on his deathbed.

If you want to know who someone is and what they're made of, talk to them on their deathbed. They have little to hide; most inhibitions are gone. Fred remained gentle and kind. He was confident in his faith in Jesus Christ. Though he had excruciating pain, Fred was dying in peace.

Fred ministered to me far more than I ministered to him. I remember leaving his home one day and thinking that Fred was modeling for me how to die. Not many young men get to see that example.

As the father of two sons, I've been intentional to teach them many things. From sports to performing arts, we wanted our sons to have exposure to many facets of life. Faith and Bible lessons were the most important lessons for our family. Plus, I wanted them to learn how to minister to others.

My oldest son, Jim, has a close friend with cystic fibrosis. This family battled that disease every day as another brother also has cystic fibrosis. Despite the disease, Jim's friend was not much different from any other kid. We treated him the same as Jim's other friends even though we had to perform breathing treatments when he spent the night.

Jim's friend was often in the hospital, which is always tough for a kid. He was usually there to take intravenous antibiotics, which is about as boring as watching rust form on car bumpers. So during one of the hospital stays, I took Jim for a visit. I wanted my son not just to see his friend, but also to see that it's okay to be in the hospital. The hospital doesn't have to be a scary place. Hospitals are places of healing, and his friend was getting better. We had a great visit, which included Jim and me praying with the family.

Later when Kim became sick with cancer, she was the focus. Our boys were seventeen and thirteen at the time of diagnosis. Each responded differently to Kim's health challenge. Whether any of us liked it or not, our family had to face up to this new reality.

During her sickness, I wanted to model for my boys how a man cares for his wife. Good days are easy, but those were difficult days. I wanted them to see that her recovery was the most important thing happening in my life. She deserved every ounce of attention and care. Real men don't ignore or abandon their spouse on bad days. Bad days are when commitments mean the most.

When Kim was sick, my father was caring for my mother who had Alzheimer's disease. He did an excellent job keeping her at home for years before admitting her to a nursing home. We spent much time at the facility on our visits home. On numerous occasions, they saw their grandfather caring for their grandmother.

With my ALS diagnosis, class was again in session. God was

giving me a chance to teach my sons a lesson that few fathers get to think about. This diagnosis allowed me to teach my sons how to die, even as Fred Howell had taught me. My resolve was to remain faithful and to focus on Kim's needs more than my own. Short of a miraculous intervention, my course was set. Kim likely had many more years to live. Her reality mattered the most.

Chapter Eight

What Changed?

AS WE LEARNED WITH KIM, the rigors and routines of chemotherapy often follow a cancer diagnosis. Soon, many cancer patients begin treatment at an oncology center. Typically, it's a room lined with recliners next to mobile pumps. The patient picks a chair, and nurses soon begin IVs with their prescription. We called the experience "the drip." The treatment can be a very social event as patients interact with one another and the medical staff. For the most part, the treatment itself is non-eventful. Most of the horror stories you've heard about chemotherapy don't start until the patient gets home.

During Kim's first treatment, she was clearly the youngest breast cancer patient in the room. Most of the women were much older, and several were on their second or third rounds of cancer recurrence. They were veterans with plenty of war stories in the midst of their attempts at encouragement.

Throughout this experience, Kim was amazingly positive and hopeful. Many found her to be an inspiration. Still, as the chemotherapy kicked in she had an unusually adverse affect that led to some difficult and scary days that brought deep levels of fear and concern.

The valley became deep and dark.

Throughout her journey, we received amazing prayer support that eventually stretched around the world. At home, we would regularly have family prayer for Kim. Particularly on the challenging days, I would pray healing Scripture over her (see Part Three). Each time we prayed with Kim, a greater sense of calm and confidence would come over her.

Because we didn't always get exactly what we prayed for, it caused some deep anguish for me. Scripture teaches that, "The effective prayer of a righteous man can accomplish much" (James 5:16). We'd submitted to elder anointing and prayer according to James 5:14. When "miracle healing" didn't occur, was it my fault? At first, the prayers didn't seem effective. What was standing in the way of prayer at this critical time? These questions led to deep soul searching and self-examination, causing me to realize that while perhaps not immediately obvious, there were areas of my life that weren't pleasing to God. The understanding that this was a heart issue first and a health issue second didn't just apply to Kim. That realization applied to me, too. Submitting to a Holy God through prayer exposed things that I would just as soon have kept covered. Adam and Eve certainly would have understood. It was like trying to put on the full armor of God according to Ephesians 6:11-17, and several pieces were missing.

Clearly, Kim was in a battle that potentially had life threatening consequences. Her first line of defense was faith expressed through prayer. Surgery and oncology became tools in the healing process. The science of cancer and all the drugs used to counter its spread become both confusing and overwhelming. In the midst of medical options and decisions, it was easy to let God take a back seat to science, forgetting that He created the very science that was doing the work of healing.

The medical care Kim received was exceptional. We grew to

know and trust the doctors and nurses. Still, there was no remorse the afternoon Kim left the treatment room for the last time. The past nine months had been like a major time out in life. Now, it was time to get back into the game.

We're not naïve. After this episode, we understand cancer and its ramifications much better. A major lesson for us was not to miss life's celebrations. After nine months in 2002 that included some very bad days, we became much more appreciative of the good days. Even on common days, there was a greater sense of joy and thankfulness. We became less guilty of taking for granted the big and little things that make life good.

Now that we're to the point of looking back on her cancer challenge, we can honestly see that as difficult, scary, and painful as cancer is, for us the cancer challenge invoked a blessing. As peculiar as that may seem, what we gained from a deeper faith and greater reliance upon God while experiencing the support of an informal prayer network that literally stretched around the world far outweighs any trauma. When we consider the consequences of Kim not discovering the lumps in her breast or detecting them later, there's cause to celebrate. It's much better to know that you have a physical challenge than to not know. That knowledge caused some lifestyle changes for both of us that have resulted in better health habits.

Cancer can do many things to a person, physically, spiritually, and emotionally. One thing it can't do is rob you of your self worth. Even while tied to pumps, losing hair, fighting fatigue, and wondering what the future holds, you don't have to sacrifice your dignity. This is where attitude becomes so important. Kim faced each challenge with a "let's get it done" attitude. Losing her hair was one of the most traumatic steps in this journey. About two-and-half weeks after her first treatment, it started falling out whenever she combed or stroked her hair. That nuisance didn't last long as she called a dear friend to our house to give her a buzz. As soon as her hair was on the floor, she slapped a wig on her head. We got three wigs before she found one that looked right on her. In the meantime, she wore colorful scarves and went about her routines both at home and in public. If people had a problem with her being bald, it would have to be their problem.

During chemotherapy treatments, there were long stretches of time when Kim didn't feel well enough to work, attend church, participate in school functions, or attend other events. When she did, she looked like a million dollars. Her appearance had changed with weight loss and a new hairstyle. The week of Thanksgiving, we visited her workplace without telling anyone we were coming. When she walked into the building, the employees didn't recognize her. Some thought she was a sales person. However, once they heard her familiar and friendly voice, they knew it was Kim. Everyone complemented her on how good she looked. Clearly, Kim had refused to sacrifice her dignity and had made the best of a most difficult situation.

Kim's cancer experience was not a walk in the park. Plenty of tears proved that—along with physical pain and uncertainty. However, the benefit of hindsight helps us put so much in perspective. That's why we share this with you, to help give some hope that one of these days cancer may make much more sense than it does right now.

From the beginning, we understood this to be a heart issue first and a health issue second. Today, we probably understand the health aspects better than we do the spiritual as we continue to discern all that God would wants us to learn.

How did cancer change Kim and our family? Our sons now have a life experience that most of their peers haven't had. They have lived with a loved one facing cancer. While each dealt with Kim's illness in their own way, each was involved in her care, particularly through prayer. As they became young men, each was able to support their friends and family who faced tough health challenges. Beyond the physical changes with Kim, it strengthened her resolve to serve others and opened a world of opportunities for personal ministry to others. She also learned her limits, and that it's ok to accept help.

How did it change me? This cancer experience changed my understanding of healing and deepened my resolve to learn more. I learned better how not to major on minors, and I deeply cherish my wife much more so than previously. We take much less for granted in our relationship. She's the joy of my life, and I thank God regularly for allowing me to share life with her.

Perhaps more importantly, I discovered a depth of emotion that had been subdued for probably forty years. Tears became a friend that allowed me to express grief and relief. My first cry came the day I announced Kim's diagnosis to my staff and other colleagues at work. That morning, a dear friend of more than fifteen years walked into my office, closed the door, and said, "I just want to hug you and pray." His embrace allowed me to release the first round of tears. It wouldn't be the last. Oddly, I did more crying after all of Kim's treatments and surgeries. When no longer consumed with her care, and after life began to return to normal, I would have moments when out of nowhere a swell of emotion and tears would rush forward. Sometimes it was while driving on Windward Parkway, while other times it would happen while speaking in public. On one occasion, I made the mistake of apologizing as I got choked up. Later, I wasn't sure why I had apologized. There was nothing wrong with the tears. At that point in the journey, the tears represented the celebration. Nothing should stand in the way of a good celebration.

A new challenge

All of the lessons learned came back to us with the ALS diagnosis. Frankly, the questions came back, too. We're human and can't help the inherent frailties and weaknesses. But this diagnosis was different. The outcome was definitive. While we made all of the necessary end-of-life decisions, we still had to live. None of us was interested in a long funeral.

The big change with the ALS diagnosis was that we had a better idea of how to cope. We immediately looked for and celebrated the blessings. When life appears to be short, there's no time to waste.

Another advantage was our faith. Without confidence in a holy God and His sovereignty, ALS might have felt like a roller coaster ride that left the tracks. I readily admit not understanding all that was happening, but I had a deep abiding peace that everything would be okay. That assurance is a gift that comes with salvation.

Along with the study of Scripture, the greatest agent of change for us was prayer. The prayer community that emerged encouraged and strengthened us.

———

There is nothing fun or easy about the topic of catastrophic health challenges. More questions emerge than answers. Rumbling in the background are scores of more philosophical questions as families deal with the inevitable why question.

In Part Two, you'll find Life Principles related to pain, suffering, and why bad things happen to good people. In the midst of a health crisis, your emotions and thoughts will likely be swirling. Perhaps Part Two will help you reconcile those emotions and thoughts.

Finally, in Part Three I share a prayer plan that God gave me during Kim's battle with cancer. Most of us really don't know how to pray during a critical illness. No matter what challenge you face, one can never go wrong when they pray the Scriptures.

Best Ideas Under the Sun®

PART TWO

Chapter Nine

Life Principles for Healing

PERHAPS NOTHING FORCES US to face life's tough questions as much as a catastrophic illness or disaster, particularly when either involves death, pain, or long-term suffering. When in our mind's eye the choice of victim seems random, we often turn to one possible common source for the cause—God. With a victim's mentality, our desire is to place blame. Whose fault is this anyway?

The questions get deeper and closer to home, particularly with a serious health diagnosis. Why me? Why now? What have I done to deserve this?

To approach these questions, it's best first to establish parameters of understanding. I call these Life Principles.

1. God's ways are holy.

Holiness singularly is the essence of God. God is set apart from evil and is pure, radiant, righteous, and glorified. He is the opposite of evil; the definition of good. "Your ways, O God, are holy. What god is so great as our God" (Psalms 77:13).

This principle speaks to the sovereignty of God. Sovereignty refers to God's supreme authority and rule over His creation. God has dominion over all of creation. The good news for us is that the all-powerful God who loves and creates us is incapable of evil. That means even when God makes tough decisions, perhaps ones that bring judgment, His purpose, ways, and means are holy.

"For as the heavens are higher than the earth, so are my ways higher than your ways, and my thoughts than your thoughts" (Isaiah 55:9). This lesson is one of the most important in life. If we chisel this lesson into the depths of our hearts on a good day, when the storms of life beat against us, we should not forget the lesson. This truth, as much as any, will sustain you during trials and challenges.

Because God is holy, He can do no wrong. During trials, it's easy to blame God. God is big enough to handle our confusion and even our anger. But that approach is a dead end. God is incapable of doing or being wrong.

When sickness or tragedy occurs, the first question is usually why. Why did I get this diagnosis? What did I do to deserve this?

The question of why is the most natural, but also the hardest. At the point you would ask why, God's ways don't feel holy. His ways probably feel punitive. While it's okay to ask God tough questions, it's best not to park on why. Instead, move on to the what and how questions. What will God teach me from this? How will this change me? The why will probably be answered in the what and the how.

Holiness drives the purposes of God. Whether creating, correcting, or counseling, His purpose is holy. Because holiness singularly defines God, it also tells us much about His ways. Being holy means that there is no presence whatsoever of evil. God is incapable of impure thoughts or hidden agendas. Very simply, the holy God that created you and me did so in His image. He created us to have a healthy relationship with Him, not an adversarial relationship. The single most important reason for our existence is to worship our holy creator. When we live in such a way that our relationship with God is strained or distanced, it's harder to trust and obey Him as we long to see and understand His purposes. But when our heart's desire is to grow in holiness, and we aim toward the goal of sanctification, the life-long process of becoming more Christ-like, His purposes are clearer because our discernment and vision are sharper. Then, trusting God is easier when we face enormous challenges.

One reason many people often struggle so much with sickness and tragedy is that their relationship to God is unhealthy or immature. Not until they experience pain or a challenge like cancer do they suddenly want to understand God's ways. That wake-up call makes you realize that a serious health diagnosis isn't particularly a curse. The good news is that God's passion and love for you is always available. Likewise, for those who try to live like Noah and walk with God (Genesis 6:9), the struggle can serve as a catalyst to deepen the resolve to be faithful. The discovery of God's mercy in the midst of a health challenge, however you might experience it, is further evidence of God's holy ways. That's how cancer or ALS can invoke a blessing that draws you closer to God.

2. Understanding doesn't begin at Ground Zero.

Within seven days of the 9-11 attacks at the World Trade Center, I stood at Ground Zero. Though the media had emblazoned the images in my mind, nothing compared to standing at the foot of the rubble. The mangled twist of concrete and metal was so huge that, even up close, rescue workers looked like ants scurrying around a mound. Even today, I struggle to describe the enormity of that scene with its sights, sounds, and smells. But one word did come to mind— iniquity. In Hebrew, it means to bend, twist, or distort. In English, it represents sin, particularly reprehensible acts of man-made evil. Sin occurs when we bend, twist, or distort God's word to suit our selfish needs. The rubble at Ground Zero was the manifestation of evil.

As in any other tragedy, I stood there for a moment and wondered why. But that answer wasn't in the rubble. That answer was in the heart of a man allegedly hiding in an Afghanistan cave. Once you understand the evil that festered in his heart and how he bent, twisted, and distorted religion to suit his purposes, you begin to understand just how possible a 9-11 tragedy is. Even worse, you realize that as long as evil has any presence on this earth, it can and will happen again.

To understand the circumstances of your life, you often need a different perspective. In business, leaders need to develop a 30,000-foot view. In other words, get a large and broad perspective first. By getting above a situation, you are better able to discern what is major and what is minor. The challenge in the midst of painful health issues is to get beyond the immediate to see the future. Is the outcome a change due to potential health limitations, or is the outcome death? And with either outcome, can we understand that the priority of the faith journey outweighs the physical journey?

Understanding often escapes us. Even at a time when the amount of information is exploding, our understanding fizzles. When faced with a personal crisis brought on by health or tragedy, we grope for understanding as we fire off questions to God, friends, and physicians in rapid-fire fashion. Perhaps deeper than our desire for healing is our desire for understanding. Confusion creates mental and spiritual anguish that can be greater than anything we experience physically.

While friends and physicians can help you with some of the answers, the understanding you long for can only come from God, as He is the source of wisdom and knowledge. Here's the instruction from His syllabus:

> "My son, if you will receive my words
> And treasure my commandments within you,
> Make your ear attentive to wisdom,
> Incline your heart to understanding;

> For if you cry for discernment,
> Lift your voice for understanding;
> If you seek her as silver
> And search for her as for hidden treasures;
> Then you will discern the fear of the Lord
> And discover the knowledge of God.
> For the Lord gives wisdom;
> From His mouth come knowledge and understanding"
> (Proverbs 2:1-7).

3. God can either allow or cause sickness.

Years ago, I worked as a staff photographer for several daily newspapers. That experience provided a great window to the world. Every day I had the chance to experience the highs and lows of life, while no two days ever seemed the same.

Inevitably, a newsperson will cover the tragedies of life such as house fires, car wrecks, or even worse. The choice of calamity often seems so random. Here's a neighborhood of homes built about the same time under the same codes, but for some reason one of the homes suddenly has an electrical problem and catches fire. Likewise, with car wrecks the victims seem simply to be at the wrong place at the wrong time. One mistake by a driver once led to more than one-hundred cars colliding on a fog-covered north Georgia interstate highway, causing four fatalities. The victims certainly outweighed the culprits on that day.

Then the day comes when you get a cancer diagnosis. If it follows twenty years of smoking two packs of cigarettes a day, then there is little to question. God allowed you to destroy your health. You're an agent of free will, and your choices have consequences. But, how do you direct connect a non-smoker's breast cancer or ALS to the victim's personal reckless behavior choices?

We sometimes fall victim to the decisions of other people. Science has now discovered that second-hand cigarette smoke is more harmful than the filtered smoke that smokers inhale. This means that smokers are forcing the consequences of their personal decision on others. Similarly, drunk drivers rarely kill drunks. Sober strangers typically fall victim to the choices of drunk drivers. However personal or private a choice might feel, every decision we make creates at minimum a ripple in the ocean of life. When ripples become tidal waves, those caught in the wake will probably get hurt.

An act of judgment doesn't cause every incident of sickness or tragic death, though Scripture teaches that God has used sickness and tragic death as forms of judgment. In Genesis 19:17, God told Lot and his family not to look back as they fled the judgment of Sodom. When Lot's wife disobeyed, she immediately died and even turned into a pillar of salt (Genesis 19:16). The consequences were the direct result of disobedience. God set the parameters and allowed the death of Lot's wife when she clearly chose to disobey.

Elsewhere in Scripture, we see that God allows hardship as a test of character and convictions. In the first chapter of Job, Satan asks God about the faithfulness of Job. Job had everything most men would want—a beautiful family and much wealth. Life was good for Job. No wonder he believed in God, Satan said. "Does Job fear God for nothing" (Job 1:9). With that challenge, God allowed the protective "hedge" (Job 1:10) to come down so that Satan could afflict Job. Satan wasted little time in killing Job's children, livestock, and destroying his wealth. Satan afflicted Job's body with boils. The hurt and misery were so great, that Job's wife said, "Do you still hold fast your integrity? Curse God and die!" (Job 2:9). Even though God had allowed this crisis in the life of a righteous man, there was no, "Why me?" pity party. Instead, Job said to his wife, "Shall we indeed accept good from God and not accept adversity?" (Job 2:10). So Job suffered though he was a righteous man. Still, the experience served a purpose that drew him closer to God.

Just as God can choose to allow calamity, He also can cause

calamity. During a pivotal time in the history of Israel, God clearly chose to harden the heart of Egypt's Pharaoh (Exodus 10:20), then chose to send a number of plagues that afflicted the Egyptians. The final plague was the "death angel" that came to Egypt and took the life of every first born, both human and animal (Exodus 11:5). By sacrificing lambs and placing lamb's blood on the doorposts and lintels of their homes (Exodus 12:7), the death angel passed over the Hebrew homes and spared them this plague while Egypt cried out in the darkness (Exodus 11:7). Soon, Moses was leading the Israelites across the Red Sea, safe from the reach of their enemies.

Perhaps the most troubling aspect of this story is why God would harden the Egyptian pharaoh's heart. Why did the plagues have to become so severe? Couldn't the result have been the same—Israel's departure from Egyptian captivity—with less pain and suffering? Clearly, God was about to do a great thing in the life of Israel after generations of captivity in a foreign land. Paradigms were about to shift and, as we later learn from the journey, they didn't shift easily during hardships. The Ten Plague-scenario, with its timing, prophecies, and fulfillment, clearly demonstrated God's sovereignty to Israel.

The prophet Jeremiah experienced his share of sorrows and understood God to be the source. In Lamentations 3, Jeremiah says that God caused his flesh and skin to waste away, and his bones to break (Lamentations 3:4) following the destruction of Jerusalem. Compared to much of the rest of this chapter, broken bones and wasted skin were minor afflictions. These were dark days for Jeremiah and the Jews. Still, though he sees God as the source of his afflictions, having allowed enemies to conquer and ruin Jerusalem, he does not turn from God.

> "The Lord's lovingkindnesses indeed never cease,
> For His compassions never fail.
> They are new every morning;
> Great is Your Faithfulness.
> 'The Lord is my portion,' says my soul,

'Therefore I have hope in Him.'
It is good that he waits silently
For the salvation of the Lord"
(Lamentations 3:22-26).

This period of Jeremiah's life was not without purpose as he modeled for the unfaithful Jews how they should seek relief from their current pain through God's mercy.

The challenge represented by this Life Principle is discerning the difference between God allowing versus causing calamity, sickness, or hardship. In the midst of personal crisis, this can be the root of one's deepest struggle. Often, we have to get on the other side of the sea before we can look back and understand the flow of events that brought us to this place. Even then, your hindsight might not be 20/20.

Unlike moral absolutes that are never changing, there are few absolutes of predictability with God's sovereignty as it relates to individuals. Yes, we can be sure of God's love and the availability of His mercy and grace. But circumstances that are unique to us and that shape how we compare to others cannot always reveal the future. Only God knows the future and how today's events will help define tomorrow.

Whatever you might conclude, don't forget to celebrate God's sovereignty at work in your life. "See now that I, I am He, And there is no god besides Me; It is I who put to death and give life. I have wounded and it is I who heal. And there is no one who can deliver from My hand" (Deuteronomy 32:39). No, it might not feel good at the moment, but through wisdom and discernment, eventually you will see evidence of God's glory through His sovereignty. Celebration will come.

4. Physical challenges and illnesses are heart issues first, then health issues.

In a loving marriage relationship, spouses want the best for their mate. If there's anything that we can do to protect our husband or wife from calamity, most of us will do that.

With a diagnosis like cancer or ALS, you begin to learn the limits of your protection. Suddenly, a challenge comes into your life that seems absolutely out of control. Very few of us would have the practical skills to diagnose or treat these diseases. The feelings of inadequacy can be enormous as you turn to medical professionals—who at first are strangers—to face perhaps the greatest challenge in your life.

There are several mile markers in the cancer journey, beginning with the diagnosis. One of those mile markers is post-operative as you await the pathology report, which is much more definitive than any medical information gathered previously. Hundreds of people had joined us in praying for the best outcome possible for Kim. I was so hopeful that the doctor's call would tell us there had been a big mistake, the tumors were gone, and there certainly was no sign of cancer. Then chemotherapy would not be necessary. We were hoping for a miracle. That report is not the news we got. The news was good and bad. There were only two tumors, not three, and they were smaller than anticipated. The tumors were cancerous, but the cancer had not invaded the surrounding tissue. However, of seven lymph nodes that were removed, one node had a micro metastasis—a tiny spec of cancer. So Kim's cancer was in more than one place. The next stop would be oncology and the rigors of chemotherapy.

That outcome was not what we wanted to hear. As we talked about the reality of not having our prayers answered exactly the way we wanted, Kim calmly said, "I've never felt this was about the body." She understood that the physical manifestation of cancer was about something much deeper than a disease. The cancer actually was a tool to fix other things.

We had already talked about this illness being a heart issue first, then a health issue. Does that seem strange to you? Does it make any sense at all? Throughout Scripture, there's a direct connect between sin and sickness. Sometimes one's behavior makes the connection obvious. Still, there are many times when it's hard to connect the dots. That's because we forget that even though some people may not engage in self-destructive behavior such as smoking cigarettes, using drugs, overeating, or sexual promiscuity, everyone fights a daily battle with their sin nature. No one is perfect or without blame before a holy God.

So in James 4:16 we find these words: "Therefore, confess your sins to one another, and pray for one another so that you may be healed…" Similarly, in Chronicles 7:14: "(If) My people who are called by My name humble themselves and pray and seek My face and turn from their wicked ways, then I will hear from heaven, will forgive their sin and will heal their land." The James passage focuses more on individual healing while the Chronicles passage is more about corporate healing of a people group or culture. Still, the pattern is consistent—recognition of sin and the confession and repentance of sin precede healing in many Scripture passages. The New Testament explains this teaching best in a story found in three of the gospels.

Jesus was teaching in a full house that included seekers, loyal followers, and detractors. A paralyzed man's friends were trying to get him inside the house, but they were unable to get through the crowd. Their desperation caused them to do something drastic. They went upon the roof of the house, removed some tiles, and lowered their paralytic friend down to Jesus. That entrance got much attention. Jesus said to the paralytic, "Friend, your sins are forgiven you" (Luke 5:20). That seems a strange response because the most obvious issue in this man's life was paralysis. How much sin could a paralytic commit?

Jesus' response was also troubling to the detractors who were present. That crowd included Pharisees and teachers of the Old Testament Law who accused Jesus of blasphemy for "assuming" that he could forgive sin. So, Jesus challenged them with this question, "Which is easier to say, 'Your sins have been forgiven,' or to say, 'Get up and walk'?" (Luke 5:23). Apparently, the Pharisees and law experts didn't have time to answer. To prove that He had authority to forgive sins, Jesus turned to the paralytic and ordered him to get up and walk. Not only did the paralytic jump to his feet, he began to glorify God.

As Jesus focused on the paralytic, spiritual issues preceded physical issues. The greater outcome was not his healing, but the glorification of the healer—Christ.

Not until this point in the paralytic's life journey can you see the greater value of his physical disability. Clearly, his paralysis became the medium through which he met Christ and found forgiveness for his sins. If you're suffering a catastrophic illness, particularly if there's much pain, this may be a very difficult point to grasp. As much as you desire to have your physical health restored, that is secondary to your spiritual health. Nothing is more important than your relationship to God. The primary purpose of your existence is to "know, love, and serve the Lord," as expressed through a lifestyle of worship, faithfulness, and obedience. Estrangement from your heavenly Father causes one to miss life's greatest blessing. If a health crisis draws that focus, then the health crisis becomes a blessing.

As Kim and I struggled with the realities of her cancer diagnosis, we felt from the beginning that cancer was the secondary issue. We weren't sure exactly what the primary issue might be, but we assumed it was spiritual. At this point that we began to realize just how much God was at work in this situation. Then we began to understand that with this cancer diagnosis, God had chosen us to become front-row pupils in His school of life. The course would be tough with many tests. But through this school, we would learn deeper lessons about Him that we might not have learned otherwise. You cannot put a price on that education.

5. The journey may be more important than the destination.

In a goal-driven culture that thrives upon achievement, the focus is often the trophy. Whether that trophy is a job, project, education, relationship, or something else, rarely will someone just hand it to you. To get from point A to point B, you have to move. The efficiency of your movement—straight line versus a crooked path—will determine the quality of your journey and the lessons you learn in the process.

When you receive a difficult health diagnosis, you likely have a number of choices. One realm of choices includes medical options. Even more important than determining a medical plan is determining an attitudinal battle plan. Will you fight to win, or fight not to lose? Will you face the future with hope or dread? Will you throw a pity party or a praise party?

What you learn in a process and how you handle the adversities of life reveals more about you than your achievements. With health challenges, trusting God is more important than your physical healing. Do you remember Job's question to his wife? "Shall we indeed accept good from God and not accept adversity?" (Job 2:10). Believing in God on the good days is easy, but what about the bad ones? The bad days prove what we're really made of.

One of the most important players in history had a colorful life. From shepherd boy to giant slayer to king, David was a man who knew God's favor yet worked overtime to blow it. Much of David's writing reflects the lessons he learned as God shaped his imperfections into something that would last throughout the ages and touch each of our lives.

The pain David created for himself and others through deceit, murder, adultery, and other shortcomings became the source of some of his best writing. "Hear my prayer, O LORD, and give ear to my cry; Do not be silent at my tears; For I am a stranger with You,

A sojourner like all my fathers" (Psalm 39:12). The pain caused David to cry out to God as he faced the realization of his broken relationship with God. The pain catapulted David from the depths of despair back into the blessed, secure arms of God. The pain made him realize what was missing.

David's journey from point A to point B was not a straight line. He made several wrong turns and stumbled often. However, the lessons he learned en route—particularly about faithfulness—created a depth of commitment and conviction that continues to teach and inspire us today.

6. Pain is not always a bad thing.

Several years ago, I injured my neck, resulting in excruciating pain that lasted for months. Numerous doctor's visits and medical procedures yielded no solid answers or relief. The pain was so great that I could not sleep lying in bed. For much of that time, I slept in a recliner.

During that time, I asked the "what if" questions. What if this pain doesn't go away? What if I have to live with this pain the rest of my life? In the midst of the pain, I didn't like the answer to either of those questions.

As I prayed during that time, God reminded me of how blessed pain-free living is. The pain gave me a greater appreciation of the good days and much hope for healing. Eventually, the pain subsided and I was able to return to a normal lifestyle. Today, I celebrate normal days more than I ever did before.

Pain is a tool. Few things will get your attention better than pain. That's why your hand burns when you touch something that's hot. The pain is telling you to get away from the heat.

Pain is a great change agent. If you're engaged in unhealthy behavior, particularly behavior that momentarily feels pleasurable, you probably won't quit that behavior until it causes you more pain than you can stand. Without pain, you might not know that your arm is broken.

Pain is a natural barometer in your life. If there's too much pressure, whether stress, the fruit of poor habits, or uncontrollable circumstances, your body's barometer indicates that change. Just as weather changes with rises and falls in barometric pressure, barometric pain is a measure that something in your life needs to change.

This understanding becomes complicated with self-induced pain, as in what accompanies alcohol or drug abuse. Not only do those who abuse suffer, but their families, friends, employer, and others experience the pain of their behavior and possible addiction. Even more troubling is when a drunk driver maims or kills an innocent person.

Chronic and perpetual pain, such as what can happen in the later stages of cancer, is very troubling. People who suffer from arthritis sometimes never feel much relief. For those people, pain probably doesn't ever feel like a good thing. Pain probably feels more like a curse or punishment. The pain, however real it might be, still becomes what you make it. Is it a barometer or teachable moment that causes you to seek the face of God? Or, is the pain cause to curse God?

7. God does His best work in a pure vessel.

My wife was a surgical technician for more than eighteen years. She helped perform thousands of surgeries ranging from tonsillectomies to open heart bypass to total joint replacements. At one point in her career, Kim knew more than six thousands surgical instruments by sight.

When rolled into a surgery suite, you go there with the assumption that the medical team surrounding you has much knowledge and experience. You expect them to understand the intricacies of the procedure they're about to perform. The surgical team has spent years gaining the knowledge necessary to perform their duties properly. Yet, one of the first things learned is among the simplest and most important. Surgeons do their best work in a sterile environment. No matter how great a surgeon's technique might be, in a non-sterile environment the patient will probably suffer infection and possibly death.

Similarly, God is the master surgeon who does His best work in a pure environment. That purity is a measure of holiness in your life. Sanctification—becoming more holy and Christ-like—is a process. We grow or decline in holiness based upon our relationship with God, which is a measure of our acceptance or resistance to the work of God in us.

God is ready to establish holiness in our life. That establishment is not something we can do. How can holiness grow out of our sin nature? The only source of holiness is holiness. God is that source. Only He can generate holiness, and the promise of Scripture is that He wants to do this in your life. "Now may our God and Father Himself and Jesus our Lord direct our way to you; and may the Lord cause you to increase and abound in love for one another, and for all people, just as we also do for you; so that *he may establish your hearts without blame in holiness* before our God and Father at the coming of our Lord Jesus with all His saints" (1 Thessalonians 3:11-13). In 1 Corinthians 6:11, we are passive in the work of sanctification: "... but you were washed, but *you were sanctified*, but you were justified in the name of the Lord Jesus Christ and in the Spirit of our God." Philippians 1:6 reminds us that sanctification is a lifelong process, not a singular event: "For I am confident of this very thing, that He who began a good work in you will perfect it until the day of Christ Jesus."

You're probably a good person. People can rely on you to obey the laws, pay your taxes, and not engage in destructive behavior. Each of us has the capacity to make conscious choices of how we will live our lives. I appreciate my neighbors who are good citizens and live in harmony. However, human "goodness" is like surgery in a non-sterile environment. Ulterior motives, guilt, duty, or agendas often infect what appears to be good. We're good because we have to be good, or because that's what others expect. The only pure source of goodness is God, whose desire is to establish His holiness in us.

Holiness is the main prescription for understanding God's ways, particularly as it applies to healing. The connection between holiness and healing in Scripture is inescapable. Christ often forgave sins before healing people as He did with the paralytic in Luke 5:20. While God is ready to establish His holiness in your life, the starting point is the identification of all that stands in the way of holiness. You cannot make yourself holy. Only God can do that. However, most of us work overtime to prevent the work of holiness in our lives. We want what we want when we want it. Not only does selfishness stand between a holy God and us, but fear also causes us to put up our guard. Before God can establish holiness in us, we've got to quit working against Him. The surrender that comes when we lay down our weapons means that we're now the property of our captor. To be captive to God means we do what He wants when He wants and how He wants it done. That obedience is scary, so we do what comes natural in the clothing of our human nature—we work overtime to resist God so that we're in control.

Most of us have this backward. We work to be good, not realizing that our good works can be an obstacle between God and us. Practicing good deeds or good citizenship is honorable, but not a substitute for the work of God in and through you. Instead, God's desire is to work through us as vessels shaped to His purpose.

The surrender that positions us to become a wholesome, God-shaped vessel begins with confession, which is when we admit to God and others that our actions and attitudes have been wrong. That admission starts spiritual healing. "If we confess our sins, he is faithful and just to forgive us our sins and go cleanse us from all unrighteousness" (1 John 1:9). Confession is the waiting room of healing, where you go before seeing the doctor.

"Therefore, confess your sins to one another, and pray for one another so that you may be healed. The effective prayer of a righteous man can accomplish much" (James 5:16). This passage also explains some of the frustration we sometimes experience in our prayer. Most of us are cruising through life without much spiritual discipline. Then a challenge like cancer or ALS confronts us and sends us to our knees. At that point, prayer is like calling a high school classmate that you haven't seen in twenty or thirty years to ask a favor. A righteous person is one who has surrendered to God's work of sanctification. Their relationship to God is close, consistent, and conformed to God's will, not their own. The lines of communication with God are much clearer for a righteous woman or man. In this passage, God is instructing the sick to submit to anointing and prayer by church elders. The intercessory prayer of righteous people can help bridge the gaps in your personal relationship with God.

Inevitably, this discussion raises the topic of holiness in the life of those who die from a major illness. Can cancer or ALS kill a righteous person? Yes. How? Why? We were born to die; it's the result of our sin nature. Somehow, we treat death as if it were the exception rather than the rule. No matter who you are or how you live, death will come.

At some point in the cancer journey, it may become apparent that the disease is terminal. For Christians, the ultimate healing comes in the presence of Almighty God. God's perspective is hugely different from ours. In light of eternity, our time on earth is the shortest period of our existence no matter how long we live.

8. God has many healing instruments and He knows when to use them.

Just as a surgeon has thousands of instruments available to him, God has more than one instrument, also. More often than not, His instrument of choice is a medical professional.

For people of faith, that may seem like a cop out. Why would an all-powerful God need people as instruments of healing? Why can't my prayer of faith heal me and keep me healthy?

Even in the recorded miracles of the New Testament, there is an important detail that is key to the healing process—touch. This happened continually in Jesus' ministry. "Wherever He entered villages, or cities, or countryside, they were laying the sick in the market places, and imploring Him that they might just touch the fringe of His cloak; and as many as touched it were being cured" (Mark 6:56). Physical touch didn't limit Jesus' capacity to heal. He had the power to heal in absentia as He did with the centurion's servant in Matthew 8.

Through the power of the Holy Spirit, common fishermen became agents of healing. Peter commanded healing often in his ministry. Shortly after Pentecost, Peter healed a lame beggar after grabbing the man by the hand and pulling him to his now formerly deformed feet (Acts 3:7). In Acts 9:34, he healed Aeneas, a man who was bedridden for eight years from paralysis.

The apostle Paul also performed miraculous healings. In Acts 14:8-10, Paul was speaking when he made eye contact with a man who had been crippled since birth. Paul could see in the man's eyes that he believed God could heal him. So Paul commanded him to, "Stand upright on your feet" (Acts 14:10). The man jumped to his feet and began to walk. Paul was God's instrument of healing in this man's life. Yet, Paul suffered an affliction that haunted him most of his life. He called it a "thorn in the flesh" (2 Corinthians 12:7). While Paul never directly identified the thorn, much evidence points toward poor eyesight while some speculate that he had a bad back. Three times in his writings, Paul says that a physician and fellow author, Luke, is traveling with him. So how can an agent of healing, who is in the company of a physician, have health issues? Only Paul can answer that.

"For if I do wish to boast I will not be foolish, for I will be speaking the truth; but I refrain {from} {this,} so that no one will credit me with more than he sees {in} me or hears from me. Because of the surpassing greatness of the revelations, for this reason, to keep me from exalting myself, there was given me a thorn in the flesh, a messenger of Satan to torment me—to keep me from exalting myself! Concerning this I implored the Lord three times that it might leave me. And He has said to me, "My grace is sufficient for you, for power is perfected in weakness." Most gladly, therefore, I will rather boast about my weaknesses, so that the power of Christ may dwell in me. Therefore I am well content with weaknesses, with insults, with distresses, with persecutions, with difficulties, for Christ's sake; for when I am weak, then I am strong" (2 Corinthians 12-10).

For Paul, the thorn was an instrument of humility that helped produce holiness. No matter how much success he might have experienced in his "career," no matter how easy it might have been to rely on his education, citizenship, or political connections, the thorn was a reminder that in and of himself, Paul was incomplete and certainly not in control of all things. The thorn reminded him to rely on God, not self, because there was no human answer for the thorn. Just as with a fast—which will surely cause discomfort particularly if it lasts forty days—brings one closer to God when accompanied by prayer, the thorn was Paul's discomfort factor that led to a good outcome that was greater than the issue of pain. Paul understood that the work of God through him was not about him. The work was about making the glorification of God evident to those who had no knowledge of their Creator. He was a righteous man through whom God revealed much about the power of holiness. However, Paul was not a perfect or complete man because of his sin nature, of which the thorn was also a constant reminder. The "thorn in the flesh" helped him keep things in perspective.

Still, the examples from the ministries of Peter and Paul point to miracle healings. Just as Jesus miraculously healed the blind, lame, and leprous people, now His apostles had healing authority. James 5:14-15 calls for the healing prayer of elders for those who are sick, following the apostles' example. Yet, most of us must admit that we've never seen a quadriplegic just get up and walk. Why don't we see more miracle healings without medical intervention?

Traditionally, there's been a theological theory that says miracles ended in the first century with the apostolic era. Therefore, God doesn't intend to reveal Himself in such a manner any more. Believing that God isn't going to do something is a great way to clog up the vessel. God's people should never impose their logic or lack of faith on an omniscient, all-powerful sovereign God. But we have. Growing out of Greek and Western thought, we practice rationalization. While rationalization serves us well in many areas of life, it doesn't explain love. Nor does it explain mercy and grace. Faith is incomprehensible to the purely rational mind. Yet God is love. He is the author of mercy and grace. Faith is His gift to us that allows us to know, understand, and follow Him.

Still, in our modern age, we expect medical answers. The technology that surrounds us is tangible. Quite simply, it's easier to trust and follow the patterns we know than to trust God for something we've never experienced.

Miraculous or divine healing can still happen today. That healing doesn't have to be a television spectacle. God, in His sovereignty, may choose to heal you in ways that are inexplicable by science.

For most, the instruments of choice will be people who are highly trained in healing skills. Just as common people relied on Peter and Paul for a touch, you and I usually rely on others. Is this wrong?

Many Christians struggle with this. Is their visit to a doctor a cop out? Is their doctor's appointment a measure of missing faith? For most, turning to the unknown is hard when you think you know so much. Trusting God seems tougher than trusting modern science. However, when you consider that all truth is a revelation of God, then you begin to take a different view of science. Whether those in the smocks and scrub clothes are believers or not, they're God's creation. God is sovereign over believers and non-believers. He's at work weaving our lives together in ways that aren't always easy to understand.

With Kim's cancer diagnosis, excellent physicians came to our aid. We felt that God clearly led us to the medical team that helped us through her health challenge. We felt the same about my ALS diagnosis.

We also saw God at work in other ways. Hundreds of family members and friends joined our journeys through prayer, encouragement, and acts of kindness. Each was an agent of healing for Kim and me. Never before had I realized how important prayer and encouragement are, particularly during tough times.

Still, the greatest healing instrument today is the Holy Spirit. I believe the Holy Spirit is still capable of divine, miraculous healing. In the sovereignty of God, I accept that sometimes healing is a process with many tools. But, I don't ever want to lose sight of the source of all healing.

9. Sin makes sickness possible.

If you want to understand all that's wrong in the world today, just turn to the third chapter of Genesis. Our understanding of human nature and divine nature begins there.

By the third chapter of Genesis, God had created Adam and Eve and had given them an incredible lifestyle. A beautiful garden. No sickness. Lots of food. Abundant love. Only one rule. Life was amazingly good, and not very complicated.

Then something happened. Eve got an idea. Wouldn't it be great to be just like God? That would be possible, she reasoned with a little outside help, if she broke the one rule. One tree in the middle of the garden was off limits. God had said not to eat that tree's fruit. To eat from that tree would bring death, whatever that was. "No," Eve heard from an uninvited advisor. "That claim isn't true. That tree won't bring death, it will bring enlightenment because the fruit of the tree in the middle of the garden will make you just like God. Wouldn't you want to be just like God and have all of His wisdom, knowledge, and power?"

Sure, Eve reasoned. Why not? Besides, the fruit on that tree looks delicious. My husband and I have responsibility over the garden and the animals. Why wouldn't that include the fruit of the tree in the middle of the garden?

So she did. Then she shared the forbidden fruit with her husband. Suddenly, everything changed. What had looked sweet and lush was actually quite bitter. They knew things that they didn't need to know. They knew things that were hurtful. Knowledge isn't always a good thing.

Their knowledge introduced a brand new emotion to the human race—shame. Never before had a human being felt the guilt or burden of shame because there'd been no sin. Adam's disobedience introduced the infection of sin to the human race. Adam and Eve knew it right away, because suddenly they became fashion conscious. Their birthday suits were all wrong, so they grabbed some fig leaves and covered their privates.

Then they heard God approaching and another new emotion emerged—fear. So they ran and hid. In their shame, they wanted as much distance as possible from a holy God. His holiness would only magnify their sin, and they each had already gotten an eyeful.

What happened next is one of the most important lessons in Scripture. In their newly created condition, God pursued them.

They're now confused, frightened, and marred. The events of this day wouldn't be easy to forget.

God pursued them in their sin state. You might think He would abandon them, but creators don't do that. Their love for their creation, however imperfect, is too great. They needed to talk.

Was God happy? No.

Did things change? Yes.

What would be different? Work would become a genuine hassle. Childbirth would become a pain. Spiritual and physical death would become a reality. God declared war on Satan, the one who deceived Eve.

Those clothes had to go because they were inadequate. God had a better plan than rotting fig leaves. Instead, He made clothes from the skin of an animal. The shed blood of a sacrificed animal allowed the sufficient covering for their newly discovered sin state. God made a promise in Genesis 3:15 that someday a descendent of Eve's would defeat Satan.

The story of Adam and Eve may be one of the first you learned as a child. Most of us are taken by the visual illustrations we've seen of this event and perhaps have never considered all of its implications. The greatest implication is that the pervasiveness of sin is so great that the simple act of disobedience in the garden didn't just change Adam and Eve, it changed humankind. The nature of humankind became infected with the capacity to want what we want more than what God wants.

Unfortunately, Adam and Eve gave birth to more than our aunts and uncles. They gave birth to sin. The effects were rather immediate as their family experienced sibling rivalry that resulted in murder.

Sin introduced pain and suffering to earth. You and I are incredibly imperfect under the radiant light of holiness. No matter how good we might think we are, holiness becomes a tough measure. If you don't typically engage in irresponsible, self-destructive behavior, it's hard to make a direct connect between sin and sickness the way one can if they smoke two packs of cigarettes a day for twenty years. Still, by the measure of a holy God, we're imperfect. Our imperfection is less obvious under the cloak of pride, selfishness, greed, or envy. Consequently, most of us go through life and never face our shortcomings.

Sin also introduced human death. Spiritually, sin is death as it separates us from a holy God. God is love, and He is life's source. Given the capacity for sin that we inherited from Adam and Eve, even at birth we're spiritually dead. While most agree that God's grace covers those incapable of comprehending right and wrong or His truths, the fact remains that even a precious child must some day come to grips with their spiritual separation from a holy God.

Spiritual death manifests itself physically. That manifestation is why our bodies at some point quit functioning, and we die. Sickness, diseases, and accidents become the pathway to a cause of death.

We typically view death with dread, particularly when it seems premature. As with most issues, God has a different perspective. "Precious in the sight of the Lord Is the death of His godly ones" (Psalm 116:15). For Christians who actively submit to the sanctification process, death is welcome as it ushers them into the presence of God.

Because sin makes sickness possible, health issues are wakeup calls for spiritual issues. While the realities of cancer, ALS, arthritis, or paralysis can consume you, please guard against the physical issues masking the spiritual challenges in your life. No matter how much pain or misfortune you face, forgiveness of sin is the most important issue. Sin issues have eternal consequences; sickness is temporal.

10. Miracles were not Jesus' primary objective.

The New Testament records more than 120 encounters that people had with Christ. Many of these include healing.

Jesus' miracle ministry began early when He turned water into wine at a wedding ceremony in Cana (John 2:1-12). In that first documented miracle, we get a glimpse of why He performed "signs" or miracles. He did this to manifest His glory as the son of God (John 2:11).

Jesus used many methods to bring healing. Whenever He chose to heal, all nature yielded to Him. His healing power was radiant, as all that many needed was a simple touch (Matthew 9:21; Matthew 14:36; Mark 3:10; Mark 6:56). Jesus covered blind eyes with mud and then pealed back the darkness (John 9:6). With a firm command, the infirm became whole (John 5:7). Even Jesus' spittle became medicine to the hopeless (Mark 8:22). In an era when medicine was much less thorough and exact as it is today, Jesus' miraculous power became the only hope that many could ever have for healing.

The first recorded miracle at the Cana wedding tells us why He would perform miracles, and that record is no accident. Throughout Scripture, we're reminded of that purpose.

In another encounter, Christ met a man who had been blind since birth. His disciples asked Him the same question that you and I ask when we or someone we love is the victim of illness or disease. What or who is the cause? This time, the disciples wanted to know if it was the man's fault (sin) or his parent's fault. "Jesus answered, 'Neither this man sinned, nor his parents; but so that the works of God might be displayed in him'" (John 9:3). In this man's life, we clearly see the sovereignty of God at work.

Jesus wasn't in the miracle business just for the sake of relieving human suffering. Jesus performed miracles to bring glory to God, His father, and to prove Himself as the son of God. Miracle healing was a means to an end.

Consequently, that's why any physical challenge that we might face isn't first about the body. Instead, it's about our relationship to a holy God, and how that relationship is established, strengthened, and deepened. Will God's glory become evident through your circumstances no matter how things look today? Or more importantly, will you give God glory in all areas of your life? The good news is that especially during your time of deepest need, God is nearby and ready to minister to you spiritually and physically. That fact is the real miracle of our Creator.

PART THREE

Chapter Ten

Prayer Plan for Healing

ONE OF THE MOST natural reactions to a major health challenge is to cry out to God. Whether in confusion, fear, anger, or hope, our prayers reflect more about us than they do about God.

With the Life Principles of Chapter Nine as background, now we turn to a prayer plan for healing. Prayer is the most powerful healing instrument available to us.

Among the privileges of prayer is your right to petition God. "This is the confidence which we have before Him, that, if we ask anything according to His will, He hears us" (1 John 5:14). And we know that, "the effective prayer of a righteous man can accomplish much" (James 5:16). What do these two verses tell us about prayer? First, a passion for righteousness and holiness will sharpen your prayers. That holiness will bring a level of discernment that will clearly help you understand what, how, and when to pray "according to his will." Accompanied by a sound knowledge of Scripture (John 5:17), your prayers will more likely be aligned with God's will. Second, the maturity that comes through sanctification and knowledge will help you better understand the "mind of Christ" (1 Corinthians 2:16), and therefore help you spend time praying in accordance with

God's will and not against it. Not everything that you would desire pleases God, and His sovereignty is undeniable. In short, God's sovereignty reminds us that He sees and understands on a scale much broader than we can comprehend.

An effective prayer plan for healing must be biblical. That's why Scripture-directed prayer is effective. Using Scripture as an outline for prayer is a practice that allows the Bible to guide your prayer on specific topics. The Scripture can give your prayer time its theme and direction for petition. There are many passages about healing. By praying through multiple passages, you'll get a broader understanding of how and when God does the work of healing.

What follows is the heart of this book, a seven-day prayer plan to direct your prayers for healing. Whether you're praying for yourself or another, this prayer plan will reveal truths about God's plan in healing. Repeat the prayer plan weekly, making it a part of your regular prayer time with God. As you repeat this prayer plan, meditating on the truths of Scripture, God will show you the depth of His Word and the wellspring of healing found there. Look into Scripture and read the stories around each day's focal passage. Write these passages on cards and keep them with you as a reminder to pray. In the Appendix, you will find other helpful passages about healing.

Scripture encourages persistence in prayer following Jesus' instruction on prayer in Luke 11:1-4. Major health challenges are formidable, and it will take much prayer to face the days ahead. Don't hesitate to invite others to pray with you about healing. While your regular prayers for healing can measure persistence, a community of praying people can help the persistence factor.

As you pray each day, think of yourself, a friend, or loved one who is sick. When appropriate, substitute the name of the one for whom you pray into the Scripture. Ask God to take the truth of that Scripture and apply it today in the life of the person who is sick or hurting. What God did for Jeremiah, Isaiah, and other people from the Bible, He can do for you.

Day One
Sovereignty

"Heal me, O Lord, and I will be healed;
save me and I will be saved,
for you are the one I praise"
(Jeremiah 17:14).

In the ancient world, choosing a god was much like a multiple-choice question as there were many options. God's chosen people—the Israelites—met constant challenges culturally from their neighbors who worshipped multiple gods. History tells us that the Jews compromised their covenant with God, which meant they were to be faithful to Him alone. Often, they embraced the pagan and idolatrous belief systems of others.

Though Christianity is monotheistic, Christians today still face much compromise when it comes to allegiance. We easily make some one or some thing our god. Jeremiah's prayer reminds us that no matter what tool God might choose to bring healing, He ultimately is the source of healing. Only God can heal, and only God can bring salvation. Therefore, our allegiance and praise, even in the midst of sickness, must be toward Him alone. God is the source of healing restoration (Jeremiah 30:17).

This verse also reminds us that we are at God's mercy. If we experience healing, it will be because of God. Likewise, we face the reality that healing might not happen as we had like. Consequently, we must learn to accept God's sovereignty as we plead for mercy.

God, I praise you as the source of salvation, healing, and mercy. No one else is capable. You alone are worthy of our praise and allegiance. Prepare my heart for your perfect will.

Day Two
Faith

"And the prayer offered in faith will make the sick person well;
the Lord will raise him up.
If he has sinned, he will be forgiven"
(James 5:15).

God's main prescription for healing is faith. Prayer is an expression of faith, and God is always listening. God wants to hear from everyone, even those who have their doubts.

The faith that heals isn't something we conjure up by getting psyched out, trying to block any possible doubt. The very faith you exercise is a gift (Romans 12:3), and it can grow. By consistently nurturing your faith, it will be strong on the day you pray for healing.

Christianity is not a lone-ranger religion. While you're singularly responsible for your actions, attitudes, and allegiance to God, you live your faith in a community, typically a local church. Then, on a day when you cry out to God for healing, the faith of those who join in prayer will support your heart's desire. In this passage, James is instructing the sick to request prayer by elders, spiritual leaders in a local church. People of faith will nurture your faith.

While God's plan is for us to grow consistently in faith and friendship with Him long before we face illness, a cancer diagnosis is often the wake-up call many of us need to rediscover and stretch our faith. When we allow God to teach us about greater depths of faith, we discover the important lessons and blessings that can come through sickness.

God, please teach me the depths of faith during this challenging time. Thank you for the faithfulness of others that surround me. Please forgive my sins and restore my soul. And may my healing be a testimony of your faithfulness.

Day Three
Countenance

"Jesus turned and saw her.
'Take heart, daughter,' he said,
'your faith has healed you.'
And the woman was healed
from that moment"
(Matthew 9:22).

For twelve years, a woman had suffered from a hemorrhage. Lacking proper understanding of her medical condition, there was little hope that she'd ever be better. Then Christ passed through her village. She was neither royalty nor a politician. There was no reason for her to have a special audience with a distinguished guest. Apparently, she didn't make a spectacle of herself. Very simply, she reached out her hand to touch the fringe of Jesus' garment as He passed through crowds (Matthew 9:20). There was something so powerful about the presence and countenance of Jesus that she had confidence in His ability to heal her.

There's no evidence that Jesus had made eye contact with her before the touch. Once He realized that she believed a simple touch of His garment could bring healing, He stopped to announce, "Faith has made you well."

The power of Christ's presence complemented her simple faith. The result was immediate healing that stands today as an encouraging testimony to us all.

God, please make the power of Christ's presence real to me today. Bolster my faith so that healing might flow from you.

Day Four
Breakthrough

"Then your light will break forth like the dawn,
and your healing will quickly appear;
then your righteousness will go before you,
and the glory of the Lord will be your rear guard"
(Isaiah 58:8).

In the midst of battles for life and health, you may ask God for a sign. A cure. A reprieve. Your hope for a breakthrough is at the core of your plea.

God's timing is perfect. In Isaiah, a breakthrough came in the midst of a humbling fast bent on worship and made evident in service. After years of defeat and brokenness in the midst of selfish pride, God stood ready to honor the contrite.

When we suffer illness or injury, pride can hinder the healing process. Instead, if we allow the challenge to bring focus to our relationship with God, humility will cause us to drop our guard. That humility positions us to experience a breakthrough that rivals a glorious dawn.

If there's a breakthrough in your health challenge, please remember that it's not for you alone. Share the breakthrough celebration with all who have loved and prayed for you. But mostly, celebrate God, the source of your new dawn, healing, righteousness, and protection.

God, prepare my heart today for a healing breakthrough that glorifies you. Teach me to submit to your ways, your will, and your timing.

Day Five
Cause

"For he wounds, but he also binds up;
he injures, but his hands also heal"
(Job 5:18).

In the long, dark days of an illness, you will inevitably ask some tough questions. "Where is God? Does He care? What difference can God make?" Ultimately, you will probably ask, "Why did this happen to me?"

That's a tough question, and you won't easily realize the answer. God's supreme authority is difficult for us to comprehend. Healing becomes an issue of faith as we trust that somehow, God "causes all things to work together for good to those who love God, to those who are called according to His purpose" (Romans 8:28). Just as an artisan takes bundles of thread and weaves beautiful patterns, God takes the threads of our lives to make something special.

Chances are, God didn't cause your sickness or pain, but he did allow it to happen for purposes far greater than you can realize right now.

Instead of asking "why," perhaps "what" is the better question. What purpose can God draw from my physical challenge? What can God teach me through this experience? And what can God teach others through me?

Be assured that God knows your pain, fears, and hopes. When struggling with God's role in health challenges, don't forget that He has plenty of band-aids. And, He is still in control.

God, teach me how to celebrate your sovereignty throughout the pain, trials, and uncertainty of my sickness. Help me not to become so consumed with why I am sick. May I learn how to see you at work in every area of my life.

Day Six
Touch

"And wherever he went—into villages, towns, or
countryside—they placed the sick in the marketplaces.
They begged him to let them touch even the
edge of his cloak, and all who touched him
were healed"
(Mark 6:56).

There are few things more comforting than the familiar touch of someone you know and trust. As a child, when your father took your hand and guided you through crowds or across busy streets, you felt safe. When fever struck, your mother's soft hand on your forehead meant that someone cared and would help you. For an elderly person who may be lonely, a visit from someone who holds their hand or even pats them on the shoulder does wonders to affirm their value while giving hope that someone does care.

An appropriate touch can be a powerful instrument of healing. Throughout Jesus' ministry, the power of His touch erased misery and hurt. Later in the New Testament, James 5:14 tells those who are sick to request anointing with oil and prayer from church elders.

The power of touch reminds us of the importance of presence in healing. Sick people need others surrounding them who care for, affirm, and encourage them. Healing rarely takes place in isolation. Whether from medical professionals, family, or friends, you need a healing touch.

The healing power of touch does not negate intercessory prayer by those who are away from you. Besides the physical touch of those near you, healing still requires a spiritual touch from Jesus through the Holy Spirit. Those around you may simply be instruments of that touch. Proximity to others doesn't have to limit the work of

Christ within you. Still, the presence of a faith community, typically found in a local church, certainly makes the recovery journey easier.

Recovery from sickness requires a healing touch. In the midst of shots, skin pricks, IVs, and oral medications, the most powerful medicine you receive may come from the warm, caring hand of someone who prays with you. As you cry out for healing, may God bless you with many people who bring the healing touch of Jesus.

God, I pray today for a touch from you that relieves my anxiety, facilitates healing, and reaffirms my worth to you and others. Thank you for revealing yourself through those who care for me.

Day Seven
Anointing

"God anointed Jesus of Nazareth
with the Holy Spirit and power,
and how he went around
doing good and healing..."
(Acts 10:38).

When Jesus ministered on earth, His purpose and assignment were clear. Jesus came to glorify God, to fulfill Scripture's promise of a Messiah, and to bring redemption and hope through a new covenant. Everything He did supported these purposes.

God anointed His son. That means God also appointed Him for a special purpose. With the anointing comes an understanding that the anointed one has the capacity to complete His purpose.

Jesus' anointing included healing power, which was a reflection of His inherent character. The healing He performed did more than relieve suffering. Jesus healed to prove the power and validity in His anointing.

Did Jesus lose His anointing in the resurrection and ascension? No. His assignment is the same today. Through the Holy Spirit, His reach is even greater today than it was in Galilee more than 2,000 years ago.

Scripture also talks about anointing as an act of healing or purification. Specifically, as you face the dark days of sickness, God instructs you to request the prayer of church elders who will anoint you with oil and pray for your healing (James 5:14). While Scripture does not teach us that this is a magic formula, it does offer an example of faithfulness and obedience that you can exercise in the midst of your health challenge. Your submission to God's biblical instruction is sure to honor the Father.

God, today I cry out for the power of healing made evident in the anointing of your son, Jesus. Prepare me for the healing work of your Holy Spirit.

One More Thing

I SINCERELY HOPE THAT *Life in the Blue Zone: God, I Didn't See This Coming* has been a resource that's helping you cope with a current health challenge.

Perhaps this book has caused you to take a hard look at your relationship with God. During that examination, you may have realized that there has never been a time when you have committed your life to Him. Or, you may have had doubts about your relationship with God because you have not attended church for many years.

Scripture teaches "that if you confess with your mouth Jesus as Lord and believe in your heart that God raised Him from the dead, you will be saved" (Romans 10:9-10). When we consciously make a commitment to God through Christ, God adopts us into His family. As a child of God, you can have a personal and dynamic relationship with your loving heavenly Father. That relationship can begin right now through prayer as you admit to God the struggles you have with sin, acknowledge Christ as His resurrected son who gives us hope over sin and spiritual death, and commit to make your new-found faith known to others.

If you'd like to talk to someone right now about how to become a Christian or how you can be sure of your salvation, please call 1-800-537-8720. People who care about you are available to talk and pray with you. They can tell you how to have a personal relationship with God through Jesus Christ.

Appendix

BESIDES THE SEVEN FOCAL VERSES in the prayer plan for healing, there're many other Bible passages that can direct your prayer for healing. The following list of themes and passages will help you pray long-term for healing. Some speak directly to healing, while others teach about prayer, faith, sin, and other topics.

Anointing
Isaiah 61:1-3
Mark 6:13
Luke 4:18; 10:34
James 5:14
Revelation 3:18

Attitude
Psalms 34:11-14
Proverbs 17:22

Authorized to Pray for Healing
2 Kings 5:7-14
Matthew 10:1; 10:8
Mark 16:17-18

Luke 9:1-2, 6; 10:8-9
Acts 5:14-16; 14:9-10; 19:11-12; 20:9-12
1 Corinthians 12:9, 30
James 5:14-15

Cause
Deuteronomy 28:61
Job 5:18
Psalms 23:4; 41:3
Jeremiah 30:17; 33:6
Colossians 1:9-12
2 Thessalonians 2:16-17

Demons
Matthew 8:16-17, 28-34
Mark 5:1-20
Luke 8:26-39
Acts 8:7

Faith
Matthew 8:2-4; 9:28-29; 17:20; 21:21-22
Mark 5:25-34; 9:17-29; 10:46-52; 11:23-24
Acts 3:1-16; 14:8-10

Friends
1 Kings 13:6
Job 6:14
Matthew 9:1-8; 25:36
Luke 10:30-37
John 5:7-9
Philippians 2:1-4
James 5:13-15;

Gift
1 Corinthians 12:9

Holy
Isaiah 58:8

Hope
Psalms 146:5-6
Psalm 147:11

Mercy/Grace
Matthew 9:12, 27-30
Acts 10:38
2 Corinthians 1:3-4; 12:9

Pleas
Numbers 12:13
Jeremiah 17:14
Matthew 8:2-3
Mark 7:31-35
John 4:46-54

Power
Luke 5:17
Acts 4:29-30

Praise
Isaiah 49:13

Purpose
Deuteronomy 32:39
Psalms 84:11-12
Isaiah 58:8

John 11:4
2 Corinthians 12:7-10

Sin
Isaiah 1:5
Matthew 9:2-8
Mark 2:5
John 9:1-7

Touch
Matthew 8:2-3; 8:14-15; 19:22; 4:36
Mark 3:10; 5:27; 6:5; 6:56; 8:22
Luke 4:26; 5:17; 6:18-19; 13:13

Word
Matthew 8:16
Luke 4:38-30

About the Author

JIM BURTON is a native of Kentucky and a graduate of Western Kentucky University in Bowling Green, Ky. Following college, he worked for daily newspapers as a photojournalist before and while attending Southwestern Baptist Theological Seminary in Fort Worth, Texas, where he earned a Masters of Divinity degree. He then spent twenty-five years working for denominational mission agencies as an editor and program director. Since leaving those roles in 2010, Jim has served as a pastor of a Korean-American congregation, freelance photographer, writer and editor, and a ministry consultant. In May 2013, he earned a Doctor of Ministry degree from New Orleans Baptist Theological Seminary, New Orleans, La.

In 1979, Jim married Kimberly Ann Ballard, his high school sweetheart. They have two grown sons, Jim and Jacob, who each live in metro Atlanta. Jim married Jadie Lizabeth Pinkston in 2010.

You can continue to follow Jim's ALS journey at www.life-bluezone.com.